The Ethical Warrior
Values, Morals & Ethics
For life, work and service

By Jack E. Hoban

The Ethical Warrior

Values, Morals & Ethics
For life, work and service

RGI Media and Publications
Post Office Box 652
Spring Lake, NJ 07762
(732) 974-7582
www.rgi.co

ISBN-10: 1475156685
ISBN-13: 978-1475156683

RGI Media and Publications is a division of
Resolution Group International, LLC

The way of the warrior is for discerning what is right for the world, enduring and training to become a moral being, becoming aware of one's destiny, and dedicating one's life to other people or the world as a whole.

- Masaaki Hatsumi, "Shinobi no Ho"

৵৵৵৵৵৵৵৵৵৵৵৵৵৵৵৵৵৵৵৵৵

Wherever I go,
everyone is a little bit safer because I am there.
Wherever I am,
anyone in need has a friend.
When I return home,
everyone is happy I am there.
It's a better life!

- Robert L. Humphrey, "The Warrior Creed"

The Ethical Warrior
Values, Morals & Ethics
For life, work and service

Introduction	Setting the Stage	1
Part I	**The Dual Life Value**	
Chapter 1	Life: The Greatest Value	27
Chapter 2	The Nature of Values	41
Chapter 3	Self and Others	75
Chapter 4	All Others	119
Chapter 5	Respect	141
Chapter 6	The Theory	169
Chapter 7	Ethics	195
Chapter 8	Activating the Ethic	211
Part II	**The Ethical Warrior**	
Chapter 9	Sustaining the Ethic	231
Afterword	Kill Socrates	299

Introduction
Setting the Stage

"My aim is not to teach the method that everyone ought to follow in order to conduct his reason well, but solely to reveal how I have tried to conduct my own."
- René Descartes 1596-1650

"All great deeds and all great thoughts have a ridiculous beginning."
- Albert Camus

The concept of an Ethical Warrior was first introduced to me by Dr. Robert L. Humphrey. Bob Humphrey was one of my graduate school professors when I was a young Marine officer at the Marine Recruit Depot in San Diego, California and taking a graduate degree at night. I had just spent the last couple of years as a series commander at the nearby Marine Boot Camp. A series commander is in charge of a recruit series consisting of approximately 320 recruits, 17 drill instructors (the guys with the "Smokey the Bear" looking campaign covers) and an assistant. Marine drill instructors have the reputation of being among the toughest men in America. Drill instructors salute the series commander, so I thought I was pretty hot stuff. My world was about to be turned upside down.

My time as a series commander had come to an end. I had been promoted to Captain and given a desk job so I could wind down from the high stress business of training recruits. Overnight I went from what was often a 24 hour responsibility to a 9 to 5 job (actually the hours were 7:30am to 4:30pm, but you get the idea). My new position consisted mostly of leading a small contingent of Marines, and signing maintenance authorizations. I was a 26 year old, highly motivated and very physical Marine officer with time on my hands—not a good combination in my case.

Although I was too young to have gone to Vietnam, I was covered under the Vietnam era GI Bill, making me eligible for assistance if I wanted to pursue an advanced degree. I was a combat engineer in the Marines, but not much of a builder of things (actually I was better at blowing things up!), so a real engineering degree didn't seem like the right direction. I decided to enroll at National University in San Diego to pursue a Master's Degree in Business Administration. I had pretty much decided to leave active duty, join the Marine Reserves and get a civilian job. Before settling down to work, though, I had a dream of going to Japan for a while and pursuing my love of the martial arts with a master teacher. It was not much of a plan, but I was ready for a change. I certainly got one—a total change in my world view.

At the university I took the usual courses needed to prepare me for the business world—finance, marketing, statistics, business law, etc. One of the required classes was titled something like "Cross Cultural Conflict Resolution in Business." To me, it sounded like one of those "touchy-feely" classes that would be a bore and a waste of time. I wondered how this milky topic could be a bona-fide course requirement. I had to take the course, but was not looking forward to it. Frankly, I was a hostile audience.

It seemed to get worse when I saw the professor. He was an older, kindly looking type, complete with the requisite tweed jacket and elbow patches. "Typical," I thought. He started by calmly interviewing every single person in the class: "Who are you?" "Where are you from?" "Why are you here?" "What are your goals?" I have to admit, there were some mildly interesting people in the class. It was post-Vietnam and the Cold War was still the backdrop for our international relations. There were a number of local business people in the class, of course, but also quite a few people from Asia (east and west). I felt little in common with most people in the class, though, as I certainly wasn't a scholar and I had never been in the real business world. My very short haircut quickly marked me as the only Marine.

The professor's interviewing went on for what seemed like hours. By the time he got to me at the back of the classroom, I was squirming in my seat. He stepped near and said, "So, you are a Marine." I remember thinking "Well, no kidding, Sherlock Holmes, look at my hair." But I threw out my pro forma, "Yes, sir." Then he smiled and calmly said, "I was a Marine, too…on Iwo Jima." Huh? Huh!

Well, if you are a Marine, a remark like that will stop you in your tracks. You probably know this (or you should), but Iwo Jima was the bloodiest and harshest battle in Marine Corps history. It is also the most famous due to the flag-raising at Mount Suribachi. Tragically, 6,825 Americans—mostly Marines—were killed on Iwo Jima (more than on D-Day in Normandy), and more than 21,000 Japanese soldiers died in the approximately five weeks of fighting. Iwo Jima arguably turned the tide of World War II in the Pacific. If you say "I was on Iwo Jima" to a Marine, you definitely have his or her attention. I can't recall what I answered about myself in my short "interview," but I remember thinking clearly that I may have severely misjudged this man. These many years later, I laugh when I think of just how wrong my first impression was of this great teacher, Robert L. Humphrey. The things he said and the stories he told during that class and later have touched me in ways that have changed me forever.

I was ready for that change. For as long as I could remember, even before I could put it into words, I had searched for the spiritual element that would round out my intellectual and physical training. When I say spiritual, I don't necessarily mean it in a religious way. I had a fine religious upbringing, including regular Sunday church attendance and parochial schooling. Instead, I mean that horizontal, people-to-people spirituality that seems so often to be absent from Monday through Saturday. A clear description of an ethic that allowed me to connect my religious beliefs more closely with my *everyday* life was what I began to hear Humphrey patiently introduce in that class.

A little background on Humphrey's storybook life is important. Bob Humphrey was a child of the Great Depression. Those were the days when life's lessons were learned in the school of hard knocks. As a child he fought for pennies in a dirt ring for the amusement of others; he later earned money as a semi-professional boxer. He rode freight trains, worked in the Civilian Conservation Corps (the CCCs), and finally joined the Merchant Marines. He transferred into the U.S. Marine Corps during World War II and became a rifle-platoon leader on Iwo Jima, where he received a gunshot-wound that ended his hopes for a professional boxing career. In combat, on that rocky island, Humphrey had his epiphany on the nature of human nature—how all relative values are ultimately subordinate to one *universal* value.

After he was discharged from the Marines he earned a Harvard Law degree and settled into teaching Economics at MIT.

During the Cold War Humphrey went back overseas to see if his worldly experiences and Ivy League education would guide him in solving

America's self-defeating "Ugly Americanism." If you are unfamiliar with this expression, it came into common usage with the publication of a 1958 novel of that name[1] by William Lederer and Eugene Burdick about patronizing and disrespectful American behavior in a fictional, underdeveloped allied country in Asia. The term "Ugly American," referred to stereotypically offensive, disrespectful, loud, boorish, and nationalistic Americans, especially ones traveling or working abroad. It was a huge problem in American foreign affairs—and still is to a significant extent today.

Over the years, Humphrey was engaged by the U.S. Information Service, the Chrysler Missile Corporation, the Army Research Office, the Marine Corps and others to improve relations between Americans and our allies overseas. He gained a reputation for being able to stop cross-cultural conflict when no one else seemed to know what to do. He taught culture-transcendent, "win-the-people" values in the most vital overseas areas—those surrounding the Soviet Bloc. In many situations his approach *did* overcome the Ugly Americanism. It *did* win back the foreign peoples. And it kept the lid on sabotage and violence in his assigned areas. In my opinion, it opened up a new social-scientific pathway to human conflict resolution.

---

[1] The Ugly American. E. Burdick and W. J. Lederer, 1958

I spent the next 16 years as Humphrey's student and part-time associate. I was amazed at his grasp of the nuances of human nature and his gentle way of explaining the "meaning of life." On Iwo Jima he had seen senseless killing and witnessed men routinely taking their turn to die. He was determined to help promote peace and harmony, and dedicated his remaining years to resolving conflict and stopping violence wherever he could make a difference.

Humphrey had a unique ability to help people and quell conflicts. He was not a theorist; he was more of a social scientist. Actually, he was a field-trained sociologist, and a researcher of human values and motivations. He taught Socratically, sharing the hard-earned lessons of his 30 plus years in the field with anyone who could benefit from his experiences and theories. His message was that there is only one vital moral interest for human beings that provides the measure of worth for all other interests, and that is the value of life. We finally persuaded him to document many of his stories in his book, "Values for A New Millennium."[2] At the end of his life he lamented that he had never really laid out the pure theory of his ideas. We talked about doing it, but time ran out. A major purpose of this book is my humble attempt to accomplish that goal on his behalf.

After 30 years of consideration, as well as reading countless texts on philosophy, anthropology, biology,

---

[2] Humphrey, R.L. Values For A New Millennium, Life Values Press, 1992. ISBN 978-0915761043.

evolution, sociology, psychology and religion, I have yet to find a theory that explains this mystery of being human as well as Humphrey's theory, which he alternately called the "Dual Life Value," the "Balanced Life Value," or simply the "Life Value." Whatever the term used, this concept illuminates human nature's most fundamental, superseding value. One of the elegant features of the Dual Life Value as a description of human nature is that it explodes the myth of moral relativism as a viable branch of ethics, yet it is flexible enough to coexist with many other perspectives on human nature and values. It can also accommodate new ideas and discoveries as we learn more about what it means to be human through the converging disciplines of science and philosophy. Most important, however, it explains how the Life Value lies at the root of our human existence—and ultimate happiness and well-being.

Another term, "core values," though fairly new, is now used quite often. It identifies certain values that a particular person, community society or organization considers important and especially applicable to them or their group. I have rarely encountered a set of core values that I did not think laudable and praiseworthy. For example, the core values of one famous (or infamous) corporation are: "Communication, Respect, Integrity and Excellence." They sound great don't they? Can you guess the company? Read on...the answer is in Chapter 7.

Yes, wonderful sets of core values are rolling off tongues and being posted lately by people, businesses, schools and organizations of all kinds everywhere. But I have noticed one common factor: they are virtually always relative. Why this clarification is important will become clear as you read this book. With all the important core values being articulated these days, there is one value that rarely makes the list. That value is life. This is so for two interesting reasons. One is because the Life Value may be so basic that it often goes unexamined or unarticulated. Another is because most people have been taught that *all* values are relative, and that is a problem.

Taking the Life Value for granted or leaving it unacknowledged—or worse, lumping it in with all of the other relative values—can (and often has) lead to conflict, fighting and even killing. The Life Value is intrinsic and has been around since the dawn of humankind. It is our only *objective* value, in that it applies to everybody—if they are alive. We need to activate an awareness of it in our lives consistently in order to be happy and to have peace. The Life Value applies to self and others and is *absolute—superseding any other relative value or trait*. In fact, the Life Value is the *core* core value. If that sounds *too* simple, please bear with me; it definitely is not, as we shall see.

This book is titled "The Ethical Warrior" in honor of those very necessary individuals in any society who possess the ethic to protect and defend. This special group of people has much to teach us about the true nature of moral behavior. Most of us have been exposed to the concept of a "Golden Rule" sometime in our lives: "Do unto others as you would have them do unto you." It is a wonderful sentiment and a challenging admonition. Yet, it is also true that the best of us go above and beyond the Golden Rule. These Golden Rule super-achievers actually do far more for others than they ever expect others to do for them. They are the most beloved and respected of our fellow human beings; they are our heroes. At the top of the hero pyramid are the defenders and protectors—particularly those who risk their lives for others. They are people of moral action who inspire us all and keep our society safe and civilized. At the *very* top are the Ethical Warriors. They protect, at great physical and emotional risk to themselves, our most cherished and universal value: Life.

I was drawn to the protector lifestyle, obviously; that is why I became a Marine. In the beginning, however, my desire to be a Marine was a vague and undefined longing for something I didn't really have words for. I was finally able to start articulating the essence of that deep attraction to warriorship due to my budding relationship with Bob Humphrey.

I also had a strong fascination with Asian martial arts. Humphrey was very supportive of my plans to further my martial arts career for reasons that will become clearer as you read on. I did travel to Japan, and I trained with a true Japanese martial arts master.

I first met Masaaki Hatsumi in the early 1980s at the home of my friend and martial arts teacher Stephen K. Hayes. Internationally renowned today, Dr. Hatsumi, at that time, was a virtually unknown *seikotsu-in*[3] bone doctor in the small city of Noda-shi outside of Tokyo. Noda City is best known as the home base for the Kikkoman Soy Sauce Company. Hatsumi taught a dozen or so martial arts students at his house. Stephen had recognized Dr. Hatsumi as a martial artist of incredible knowledge and ability and had invited him for his first visit to America. Dr. Hatsumi had been trained by the "Mongolian Tiger," Toshitsugu Takamatsu, and inherited from him the grandmastership of nine different schools of ancient Japanese martial arts. These schools trace their roots back more than 1000 years to an extremely remote and mountainous region of Japan named Iga and include unconventional skills of armed and unarmed combat, scouting, spying and commando assault—perfect for a Marine! When I left active duty I went to Japan to train directly with Hatsumi Sensei. I have studied consistently with him for more than 30 years.

I once asked Hatsumi Sensei, "What is the purpose of martial arts?" He replied: "Life." At that time I thought his answer was an answer to some Zen

---

[3] Seikotsu is a Japanese style of osteopathy-like massage and exercise therapy. It is used to treat a wide variety of injuries.

koan[4] that I didn't know I had asked—or perhaps just an example of the man's inscrutability. It took me years to realize that his answer had actually been clear, direct and literal—perfectly consistent with Humphrey's Life Value theory.

My atypical combination of values training and martial arts has made for a very satisfying life in most ways, yet a frustrating one in others. You will soon read about some of my adventures—and misadventures. The most satisfying parts of the journey have been two-fold: I have met so many interesting and good people all over the world who live a life of hardship, danger and service—the warrior path. Their selflessness and sacrifice are simply humbling. I have learned from them, trained with them, and have had the opportunity to share the little I know with them. They are simply awesome.

A second source of satisfaction is more specific. I am privileged to serve as a Subject Matter Expert (SME) for the United States Marine Corps Martial Arts Program (MCMAP). In 1996, the Commandant of the Marine Corps, General Charles Krulak, convened a Close Combat Review Board (CCRB) at the Marine Corps Base in Quantico, Virginia. A number of SMEs were assembled to represent various perspectives on close combat, and I was pleased and flattered to be among them. Our mission was to

---

[4] A koan is paradoxical question posed to a student of Buddhism for which an answer is demanded; the stress of meditation on the question is intended to spark enlightenment.

review the Marine Corps doctrine on close combat
and recommend revisions—or if necessary, an
overhaul—of the program. It was a lively group that
included a World War II veteran whose time with the
Office of Strategic Services (OSS) had made him an
expert in silent killing techniques, various Marines
known for being experienced martial artists, and
several men who had worked in the dangerous field
of personal protection after serving as Marines. I was
invited because of my reputation as a Marine martial
artist and longtime student and practitioner of
Japanese battlefield arts. I was also representing Dr.
Humphrey, (who had killed an enemy solider with a
rifle butt stroke while serving as a Marine rifle
platoon commander on Iwo Jima). Humphrey, a
confidant of General Krulak, was too ill to attend, and
passed away shortly thereafter.

We were a fairly collegial group, and sincerely
dedicated to making recommendations that would
adequately address the necessary close combat needs
of Marines in the relatively new era of Low Intensity
Conflict (LIC). A sense of cohesion and shared
purpose developed gradually over the course of that
week due in part to some after-hours training sessions
sponsored by one of the men. In those sessions, we
shared a gritty, no-nonsense training experience. That
small dose of "shared adversity" broke down some of
the natural barriers between us and created a warrior
bond. Training together—as opposed to talking and
debating—tends to do that.

That is not to say that we all were singing from the exact same sheet of music. We weren't. As the week progressed it was clear that there were at least two fundamentally different viewpoints on the approach that should be taken in revamping the close combat program. This may be an oversimplification—and it certainly is a personal point of view—but it appeared that one group felt that the objective was to compile a catalogue of the most vicious and effective hurting and killing techniques in history. In their view, this new close combat system should be designed to make Marines the most feared close combatants the world has ever known. Although we were all mostly on board with the new program being tough and effective, there was another group whose perspective was also focused on the ethical issues of close combat.

Was it possible for the new program to provide all the skills needed along the entire continuum of force, while also producing Marines who were the epitome of moral behavior—modern day warrior knights? Although the idea of an honorable and ethical Marine was appealing, there were a number of people who felt that including "values-training" in the curriculum was outside the scope of our mandate. They also feared that such training could possibly, in the context of the realities of close combat, put Marines at risk by making them hesitant or "soft." This was, indeed, a valid concern. We left without truly integrating ethics into the curriculum.

Our findings and recommendations went through the usual vetting and revisions (I recall receiving draft copies at various points between 1996 and 1999), and eventually resulted in the Marine Corps Close Combat Training Program (MCCCT). There is little mention of the ethics discussions that occurred at the CCRB in the manual for the program, MCRP 3-02B. In my opinion, the lack of an ethical component is one of the reasons why the MCCCT was superseded by the Marine Corps Martial Arts Program. We have since learned (or re-learned) that warriors need more than physical techniques to prevail in close combat. The proper, tough combat mindset is vitally important— that is, an ability to think clearly and tactically under stress.

Marines must also have the ethics of a warrior. These ethics ensure that Marines act in accordance with the Marine Corps core values of honor, courage, and commitment as they apply close combat techniques as protectors of our nation. Ethics without the physical skills may not make an effective Marine, but possessing these powerful physical skills without ethics may create a thug who would use them inappropriately, thus bringing shame and dishonor upon the Marine Corps and our country in an era of extremely delicate Counterinsurgency (COIN).

In introducing the Marine Corps Martial Arts Program to the Corps in 1999, Commandant General James L. Jones stated that "as every Marine is a rifleman, every Marine shall also be a martial artist." MCMAP, today, is a synergistic regimen of physical training, mental training and values-activating "tie-ins," or stories. Tactically, MCMAP is a weapons-based combatives system and, as such, has evolved into the finest and most complete martial arts program ever introduced into the Marine Corps. The physical aspects of the training—combat conditioning and armed and unarmed martial arts techniques—have become a familiar sight around the Marine Corps as participants practice the MCMAP techniques in their quest for the coveted "next belt" in the system. MCMAP is not a sport; it is a close-in warfighting system conducted in combat gear—including flak jackets and Kevlar helmets, when possible. MCMAP was not developed for use in competitions or other sporting events that have the purpose of deciding a personal "winner." MCMAP employs a "Marine team" approach designed to facilitate the winning of wars against our nation's enemies, capturing or killing the enemy when necessary, while allowing Marines to effectively protect innocents, each other and themselves, whether it be in combat or at home. Significantly, the core of the Program is considered to be the values or "character" aspects. MCMAP develops "Ethical Warriors." This emphasis on moral values—including the Marine Corps core values—further differentiates MCMAP from any other combatives program in existence today.

One of my tasks as an SME is to help clarify the concept of an Ethical Warrior and share it with the Marines. Even after years of research, completely satisfying definitions of terms like "values," "morals" and "ethics"—at least ones that were useful for our purposes—still eluded us. This may be due to the atmosphere of ethical relativism in our institutions of higher learning or (even more likely) because certain aspects of human nature are just so hard to describe in words. Therefore, this book draws heavily on Robert L. Humphrey's experiences and writings. His work filled in many of the blanks.

I must be clear in saying that, aside from my work with MCMAP as a subject matter expert or consultant, I have not been an active duty Marine for a long time (however, I am still a Marine—once a Marine always a Marine!). I have never been a full-time martial arts teacher, either; although I have trained most of my life, teach a local training group in my community, and have done hundreds of seminars in the U.S. and around the world.

Nor am I a scholar or philosopher. So you may be asking, "Well then, what have you been doing all these years?" The answer is simple; I have had a "day job." I have spent much of my career as a sales and business development executive in a variety of industries that include healthcare information technology and business process outsourcing (BPO). The corporate arena and business world are full of good people and some bad people. There is challenge and adversity in business and the marketplace can be a type of battlefield at times. I have struggled, sometimes mightily, to apply the code of the Ethical Warrior in my life and business. My results have ranged from "excellent" to "needs more work," with a couple of "crash and burns" thrown in the mix. Yet, I have seen the Dual Life Value operate inexorably in all encounters between people in all circumstances — including the business world. If you are a business executive reading this book, know that the principles of the Ethical Warrior apply directly to your challenge of staying ethical in the highly competitive, and sometimes adversarial, world of commerce. You will be able to connect the dots easily.

The Dual Life Value also applies in personal relationships. Most of us have many roles in life. In my case, along with everything else, I am a family man with a wife and two children. The pressures I have felt in raising a family, including the difficulties in "practicing what I preach" within my own "in-group," inform this book. My experiences and the pleasurable challenges of instilling moral values in the next generation as a father and coach, I hope, will be of some inspiration to the reader as well.

In writing a book that draws both from the world of war and the world of ethics I must be clear in stating that I am no longer of the age to fight in the current day conflicts. Sun Tzu, in his seminal work, "The Art of War," wrote that a great general is one who finds a way to win without fighting a single battle. I have never (except for several personal skirmishes) fought a single battle. I am sure that this does not make me a great general, but it does give me a certain objective perspective regarding war and killing that has proven useful.

As for ethics, if I had not met Bob Humphrey, I probably would have no more of a road map to moral behavior than anyone else who merely struggles to "be a good person" and "do the right thing" every day.

This book, therefore, is not only for Marines; nor is it just for law enforcement officers and martial artists. It is for *you and me*. In a nutshell, I am basically an American working guy who has had the good fortune to be exposed to great mentors of outstanding moral character, experience and knowledge. I have struggled to understand the essence of their profound ideas while simultaneously trying to live according to them. I have observed that the hallmarks of their lives have been outstanding service to others, resulting in a high level of personal happiness and inner peace. I have used their stories for inspiration, and am passing them on in my own way. I have tried to clarify the philosophical elements of their great lessons so that I could use them in my own life. I share them now, not only for use under the stress of war and other great adversities, but in everyday life. After all, the difference between right and wrong (morality and immorality) is not often a matter of life and death. Sometimes it is just a matter of attaining and maintaining a good life—doing the "right thing." Yet, the Life Value insights and principles, forged in combat, are amazingly instructive for those who will never hear a shot fired in anger. It is clear that the ethic of the warrior concerns the human condition—and life itself. As you read this book, don't think that it is about someone else. Think: *it is for me.* Because it is, and that is why I wrote it.

The first 6 chapters of this book are for everybody, as they cover the Dual Life Value Theory from many angles and perspectives, although those in the protector professions will find much that applies specifically to their vocation. A quick word about redundancy in the book: it is purposeful, so please bear with it; I have found that the concepts discussed herein are simple, but extremely subtle, and bear repeating.

Chapter 7 deals with the Dual Life Value as applied to work and business. Chapter 8 talks about education. I urge those in the protector professions not to skip these chapters, as we all have to deal with the business aspects of life; we are also teachers—as parents, coaches and, perhaps, even instructors in our professions. Many of us have children who attend America's schools—both public and private.

Chapter 9 is for the Ethical Warriors and Ethical Protectors. However, the concepts in this chapter are worth exploring, even if you are not in the protector professions. Please read them.

The Dual Life Value, as an intellectual concept, is fairly straightforward, but its manifestation in the many different situations we encounter in life is sublime. Following the Life Value is a rocky and winding road, sometimes with two steps forward, and one step back. There are some dead-ends, some switchbacks, many uphill climbs, and a few downhill coasts. And, the road never ends. Humphrey called it "the high road," and it is a good life. It benefits the traveler, and everyone he or she encounters on the journey. However, for you do-gooders out there (and I consider myself as much of a Don Quixote as anybody), here is an insight for you: Saving the world is like mowing the lawn; you have to do it about once a week. Be patient and persistent with yourself and others.

I believe that the Dual Life Value is a very satisfying articulation of human nature. However, I realize that saying "life is our superseding value," as a strictly intellectual declaration, may seem overly obvious and not completely helpful. But, I would then ask: If life *is* such a universal and obvious value, why do we humans kill and disrespect each other constantly? Merely saying that life is our most important value is not enough to assure that it is always acknowledged as such.

Three other elements are important. The first is a clear understanding of the nuances of how the Life Value drives all of our decisions and actions. This clarification is necessary and very interesting.

The second is an ability to "feel" the Life Value deep in our "guts," deep in our conscience—consistently and under stress and adversity. One of the devices Humphrey used to activate these feelings in his work was values stories. Several of the exact stories he used in his teachings are included in this book in addition to some new ones of my own.

Point three is *practice*. The deeply satisfying feeling of being ethical can wear off—particularly under stress—without a method of sustainment. Humphrey used a combination of the values-stories and a modified version of boxing to sink the lessons deep into our psyches. Boxing? Later in the book, I will spend some time explaining why we used boxing. Now, we use martial arts—although you need not be a martial artist to practice being ethical.

One of the limitations of this book revolves around the fact that no methodology for developing Ethical Warriors is complete without total emotional activation, as well as, a physical training regimen. *Doing* is the key. You can read all the books you want; it's not until you feel it, try it, taste it and embrace it that you'll really capture a full understanding. The process of understanding the Life Value concept starts off a little like that first look through an unfocused telescope. Although everything is right there through the eye piece, it is all extremely blurry. But as you slowly start to turn the focusing dial, things get clearer and clearer until the view is unmistakable. Your Ethical Warrior training is like turning the dial: as you practice, things will get clearer.

When we teach the Ethical Warrior or Ethical Protector courses to Marines, law enforcement officers and other conflict resolution professionals, we utilize a multi-day integrated and "three-dimensional" course of instruction designed to clarify, activate and sustain a healthy balance of regard between self and others:

- Clarity: What is humankind's most important value and why?
- Activation: How do I get the sense of it, deep in my conscience, deep in my "guts?"
- Sustainment: Once I get the feeling, how do I keep it from "wearing off," especially under stress, but also in everyday life?

The process covers the "ethical, verbal and physical" aspects of being a skilled conflict resolver. I obviously can't transmit the entire Ethical Warrior experience in a one-dimensional or, if we count the stories, two-dimensional medium like this book. The piece that is obviously missing is the "doing" part. But are you intrigued? Do you like the sound of the expression "Ethical Warrior?" Would you like to attain the nobility and confidence that is attainable for all of us as human beings? I can't give you the whole training methodology herein, but I can try to give you a lot of it. Interested? Then, please read on.

PART I

The Dual Life Value

Chapter 1
Life: The Greatest Value

"All truths are easy to understand once they are
discovered; ...the authority of a thousand is not worth
the humble reasoning of a single individual."
- Galileo

"I'm not smart. I try to observe. Millions saw the
apple fall but Newton was the one who asked why."
- Bernard Mannes Baruch

"The more original a discovery, the more obvious
it seems afterward."
- Arthur Koestler

What is humankind's universal and superseding
value? As presented in the Introduction, it is the Dual
Life Value—a balanced regard for the lives of self and
others. But, living according to the Life Value is not as
simple as saying it. When I start explaining it to
people, I often hear things like: "I always knew that, I
just didn't have the words for it." This begs the
question: If we all know this, then why do we need to
"learn" it? The reason is because, although we *may*
know it, we often lose sight of it. And that causes
problems for us and for others—big problems. The
good news is that, with a little clarification, activation

and practice, we can live happier, more balanced lives.

Today, we live in a connected and shrinking world of modern marvels. We can travel almost anywhere on the planet at a moment's notice, and we can communicate instantly with billions of people over the Internet. In many ways we are all coming closer together in ways that were unthinkable a few short decades ago. Yet our world, in other ways, can still resemble the "Dark Ages" in terms of ignorance, fear, hatred and violence. These terms apply, to some extent, to all sides in the various conflicts that we see worldwide—internationally, of course, but also within our own countries and communities.

We may want to do something—but what? It reminds me of the story of a man standing in front of his home in a bathrobe one night as the house is furiously burning down. A neighbor runs up and yells, "How can you just stand there and let your house burn down?" The man turns to his neighbor incredulously and says, "I'm not letting it burn down; its burning down on its own." A practical person realizes that we just can't do anything about some bad things. So let's stay realistic.

However, even though there is ample evidence of injustice and war almost everywhere we look, when seen in context, it might also be argued that things are getting better. There *seems* to be a lot more violence today than in the past, but is that really true? Let's not confuse numbers with percentages. There are a lot more people on the planet today than there ever have been—more than 7 billion! The number of conflicts may be up, but the percentage of people engaged in or exposed to violence is probably way down. Certainly instances of international aid and charity during natural and man-made disasters are off the charts. So why does it still feel like the world is getting more dangerous? Pervasive media is one reason, of course. We hear a lot more about the bad things that happen in the world than the good things. We also continue to fear the possibility of nuclear war—although we seem to be going through a stage where "small wars" are the norm.

The root of the possible misconception is also philosophical. Unsubstantiated and largely debunked theories of human nature (or the lack of one) "inform" us that human beings are merely "noble savages" who have been waylaid by modern technology, making us more violent and dangerous. Some people propose that if we could somehow go back to a more "natural" way of living, things would be simpler and better. Other perspectives claim that man is inherently selfish, immoral and evil and the new technology will just make it more pervasive.

The truth is that the life of man for millennia, as Thomas Hobbes said, was "solitary, poor, nasty, brutish and short." Did you hear the one about the caveman talking to his friend? "We live an absolutely natural lifestyle and eat only organic foods. So, why is our average lifespan only 38?"

Today life is pretty good for billions of us on this planet and getting better. It is hard not to acknowledge that something is driving us to improve the state of human existence—our own and that of others. Though the technology of violence has become scarier and more powerful, so too has the technology for peace and well-being. Think about it: would you rather be a medieval king, enemies everywhere, freezing in a castle or a middle class (even lower middle class) John Doe living in a warm, electrified and sanitary house, eating easily obtainable food, enjoying 24 hour entertainment, with emergency healthcare or police protection just a 911 call away? Let's be real, I think most of us would take the latter.

That is not to say that there isn't a lot more that can be done to resolve conflict and promote peace and well-being. There is. Yet, the secret to a happier, more peaceful world already lies within almost all of us.

There are tremendous discussions going on in sociology, biology and psychology about whether the nature of man is social (learned) or biological (in our DNA)—or some combination. The most important of those arguments surrounds the question of whether man's nature is a "blank slate," written on by his experiences and environments; or if human nature is "innate" and only influenced by our genetic differences, the environment and our social interactions. This book proceeds from the premise that, in addition to our "environmental conditioning," there is an innate human nature with foundational values that are "hard-wired into us." When they are acknowledged and acted upon, the lives of all people improve; when they are not, we suffer. There is one simple, yet sublime value that is primary to human nature and a requisite to human happiness and harmony. That is the Life Value.

My friend, the late Dr. George Thompson, creator of the very effective Verbal Judo[5] method of conflict communication, used to say: "all action flows from a philosophy." I would add: "whether or not you know what that philosophy is." The Dual Life Value, as a concept, is really a philosophical clarification of the nature of human values. How do we not know—and act consistently according to—our own deepest nature? Perhaps, because the essence of our human nature is subtle and often taken for granted, either consciously or subconsciously, people act based on their values. However, we have many values and some are not always reasonably prioritized.

One purpose of this book is to help clarify the Life Value in the context of the concept of an Ethical Warrior for use by all of us. We will discuss effective ways to activate it in our consciences, and sustain it consistently in our actions through practice. Do you have to be a "warrior" to benefit from this book? No, but you probably do have to have a desire to be an ethical person in *your* life and vocation.

Before we actually try to clarify the Life Value concept, it is extremely important to note that understanding it perfectly from a philosophical perspective is not as important as living according to

---

[5] Thompson, George. The Verbal Judo Way of Leadership, Looseleaf Law Publications, 2008.

it. Consider breathing. Knowing the physiological details behind the magic of taking in air, utilizing the oxygen, and expelling carbon dioxide, isn't critical—unless there is a problem. Then a thorough understanding can be *very* helpful—along with, perhaps, the services of a pulmonologist.

The "delivery method" we have used to clarify, activate and sustain the Life Value in self and others—and develop Ethical Marine Warriors—has been the physical regimen of the martial arts. When I say martial arts, I am not limiting it to the Japanese martial arts I study, or the Marines' MCMAP program. Other martial styles, including boxing and wrestling, presented in the proper context (with the clarified ethic and values-activating stories) may be sufficient to activate the Life Value. Later in the book we will discuss a modified boxing program called STRIKE that has worked very well.

Let me also be clear in saying that you *don't* have to be a martial artist to be ethical. Other sustainment programs may also work as long as the content and tone of the training are consistent with the principles that we will discuss. But you do have to be a "doer," and that takes physical self-confidence.

Before moving on, however, a word of caution is in order. There is a tendency for people to explore a topic like ethics from a predominantly intellectual or philosophical point of view. But, it is probably not an exaggeration to say that it is a *waste of time* to read this book and then sit around discussing it. You will need a tangible way of practicing both the moral and physical aspects of the methodology. The physical and the moral disciplines combine to give us the world of ethics.

Ethics may seem to be a field reserved for the realm of intellectuals, but it is not. When subjected to great adversity or violence we are often required to act (or react) quickly and without time to think. But *what* will we do? From what values will our actions flow? Remember what Dr. Thompson said: actions flow from our value system, whether or not we have examined and clarified it beforehand. Adversity may call for great moral and/or physical courage and, so, reveal our deepest values. Adversity may also reveal our character flaws. By practicing a clarified value system in everyday life we can strengthen our character in preparation for the challenging times.

As we explore these complex and varied topics, note that the same fundamental values used to train and develop Ethical Warriors can work for all of us as we deal with our own adversity and conflicts in life. The lessons are clear and accessible to everyone with a capacity for moral action.

The word "ethics" comes from the Greek word *ethos*—and roughly translates to "moral character or custom." One of the goals of this book is to provide a coherent vocabulary for the terms "values," "morals," "ethics" and associated concepts. Briefly, a "value" refers to that which we seek to gain or keep because we consider it to be of worth. It can be a tangible like money or material possessions; it can also be an intangible, like a feeling or belief, etc. "Morality" refers to "good" values. "Good" means "respectful of life and that which protects and sustains life." Ethics are "moral values in action"—or moral conduct or right behavior. We'll expand on those definitions later, as well as, the critical difference between relative values (values that are subjective or environmentally-driven or a matter of preference, custom or opinion) and our Life Value (which is an absolute and inherent value, and so important for virtually all of us that it is literally a matter of life or death).

As presented in the Introduction, I have lived at an interesting and fortuitous confluence of values and action, having been exposed to two extraordinarily moral men who were also thoughtful and physical. Their lessons, in combination with my own experiences and subsequent study, have revealed a clearer view of human nature—and how acting in accordance with that view is a recipe for a happy and noble life. The bottom line is that we can all benefit from a clearer understanding of human nature, and we can learn to better activate the Life Value in our hearts and consciences to reap that benefit. This self-knowledge will help keep us from straying from our own human nature in ways that would ultimately result in unhappiness for ourselves and others.

It can also protect us from unethical people who would harm us. Moral clarity guides us objectively in recognizing as wrong the actions of persons who violate the rules of human nature and the Life Value. They must be avoided, confronted and/or stopped, because their actions are a danger to the rest of us. While trying to be a "good" person, we must also recognize that there are some "bad" people out there—and it is not just a difference of opinion. Part of living a good life is having the courage to deal with immoral people—or at least the immoral actions of some people. We must learn to recognize unethical behavior for what it is, and defend ourselves against truly immoral—evil—people. We all run into them at one time or another in our lives.

I remember patronizing a small restaurant with my good friend Mark Hodel many years ago in the Chiba prefecture of Japan. Mark and I often went there after training to relax and flirt with the girls who worked there. The place was run by a husband, wife, and their four daughters—one of whom I thought was exceptionally cute. On this particular night it was a bit late, but the place was still full with patrons eating and drinking, as were we—mostly drinking. Suddenly it got very quiet and the temperature in the restaurant seemed to drop about 10 degrees. I looked around to see what had happened, and the cause was obvious. Two men had entered the dining room. One was an older man with a big smile that revealed a mouthful of gold teeth. The other man was a very large, thuggish looking guy in a painted-on polyester suit and a big bulge under his jacket. I had heard that Chiba was known to be the home turf for the *yakuza*, Japanese mafia. These guys definitely seemed to fit the bill.

Mark and I looked at each other tensely. These two characters assiduously ignored us. "Polyester man" went around from table to table, whispered something, at which point the people dropped their chopsticks, got up and left, one by one, until the place was empty. Meanwhile "Goldy" had gone back into the kitchen where he started pinching the girls' butts and rifling through the cash register. Not being too bright (or sober) I got pissed and started to get up to do...I don't know what. Mark, of cooler head, grabbed me and urged me to calm down and wait to see what would happen. Finally, "Polyester man" sat down at the bar facing our table, started drinking tea and staring at us with a blank expression. "Goldy" came over with a false smile on his face and asked, rather aggressively, what Mark and I were doing in Japan. The girls were peeking out from the kitchen with nervous looks on their faces; Mom and Dad were standing behind them wringing their hands. Thinking unwisely to myself "Hey, I'm from New Jersey, don't screw with me," I told him we were there to practice martial arts and what of it? "Goldy" sneered and asked, "Where?" I said "Here, in Noda." He smirked and said, "Yeah? With who?" I said "Hatsumi Sensei."

Suddenly, everything turned on a dime. "Goldy" was smiling again, calling for more beer, and putting his arm around me. "Hatsumi Sensei! Why didn't you say so?" "Well," I was thinking, "I just did, you jerk."

But, relieved, I didn't say that, and just smiled along. Breathing his ugly breath in my face he started speaking in Japanese, some of which I didn't understand, but the gist of it was that Hatsumi Sensei was his *onjinsan* (benefactor) and had saved him from an assassination attempt. He owed Hatsumi Sensei his life! Huh? He gave me his card and it turns out his name was Shima (I found out later he was known as Shanghai Shima, supposedly for some atrocious killings he had committed in China during World War II). Anyway, Shima and I were now buddies and he said he was going to take me and my friend out on the town. I said, "Sure," and poor Mark groaned. Shima just had to make a toilet call first. He headed to the men's facility and as soon as he shut the door, the girls ran in and whisked Mark and me out the back into the alley where their car was running. They drove us back to the inn where we were staying and begged us to keep the whole matter quiet.

Well, I couldn't control my curiosity, so the next day when we were at Hatsumi Sensei's house I casually mentioned that I had met a friend of his the night before. Sensei said, "Oh? Who?" I handed Sensei the business card that Shima had given me. Hatsumi looked at it and laughed. "Ha," he said, pointing at the card, "This guy is a yakuza; I saved his life." I said, "Yes, he told us that." Still looking at the calling card, he said softly, "He is my friend." Then he looked up at me with a mysterious smile and said, "Chief of police, also my friend." There was a lesson there that I have not forgotten.

Aleksandr Solzhenitsyn once wrote: "If only there were evil people somewhere insidiously committing evil deeds, and it were necessary only to separate them from the rest of us and destroy them. But, the line dividing good and evil cuts through the heart of every human being. And who is willing to destroy a piece of his own heart?"[6]

Hatsumi Sensei's "friends" on both sides of the law—and Aleksandr Solzhenitsyn's admonition—makes it clear that that we all have some good and bad in us. But I would also like to add that nearly everyone does have a moral sense at the core. The vast majority of people do understand right from wrong—intrinsically, in their "guts." Their feeling of respect for the life of self and others—morality—is inherent and deep. So if you want to "learn" or "teach" moral values, it is helpful to know that, rather than just being "taught," moral values can be clarified and "activated." Moral action, happiness and well-being become a natural, consistent state of existence for all of us—the rule rather than a mysterious, sometimes fleeting, exception. I say "all of us," but it is true that there is a minority of people, perhaps one to four percent,[7] who do not respect life as the rest of us do, and we will explore that briefly in later chapters. At this point, let it suffice to say that immoral acts are immoral because they are the

---

[6] Solzhenitsyn, Aleksandr I. The Gulag Archipelago, 1918-1956: An Experiment in Literary Investigation (Volume One). pp 168.
[7] Threshold: The Crisis of Western Culture. T. Hartmann. Viking 2009. Ch 5

exception. It is precisely because one bad apple *can* spoil the whole barrel that we call it bad.

Sometimes people lose sight of the Life Value due to traumatic circumstances. Extreme violence and death is shocking and disorienting. Strong emotions such as fear and anger can cause us to over-ride our nature. If a soldier became temporarily stressed to the point that his or her ability to differentiate between right and wrong was confused due to the "fog of war" it would be extremely regrettable, but perhaps understandable (although not excusable).

In the course of everyday life, we also may experience great stress and adversity that tempts us to do the wrong thing. The path to moral behavior can also become obscured merely due to a laziness of the conscience, or from being confronted with confusing and strange cultural values, customs or behaviors. Bullies are another intimidating distraction. All of these things can cause our moral compass to malfunction so that we lose our natural inclination to do the right thing. Moral clarity can also "wear off" due to a lack of "exercise," or attention. The ability to act with moral consistency, particularly under very stressful conditions, requires clarification and activation. A sustainment program or *practice regimen* is the final—and crucial—element.

There is a good amount of well presented material on the subjects of values, ethics, cross cultural conflict resolution, etc. The best of this literature is useful, perhaps vital, in fleshing out the ideas presented herein. But it is also clear that a purely intellectual or scholarly approach is not enough and that the literature is missing some necessary philosophical elements. Many of us are neither scholars nor intellectuals. Most of us are not Marines for that matter. But we can benefit from exposure to the philosophically clarified values of an Ethical Warrior. For the record, many Marines—perhaps most—are no more moral than the rest of us. They are just patriotic, and sometimes heroic, young men and women, who have answered that indefinable "call to duty." Experience has shown that a clarified value system activated using the methods discussed in this book, and sustained by an effective physical-moral training regimen, is successful in developing Ethical Warriors—and everyday people—of good character. In other words, the approach works for almost everyone. Though we will explore some important philosophical points in an effort to facilitate a better understanding of our human nature, I have found that a curriculum to help develop character and moral behavior doesn't have to dot every philosophical "i" and cross every intellectual "t" to be effective. Most people are basically moral already; sometimes ethical proclivities just need a little activation.

Chapter 2
The Nature of Values

"There is only one moral, as there is only one
geometry."
- *Voltaire 1694-1778*

"Relativity applies to physics, not ethics."
- *Albert Einstein*

"Ethics is nothing else than reverence for life."
- *Albert Schweitzer*

"I say no wealth is worth my life!"
- *Iliad 9.401-409, spoken by Achilles*

In this book, human nature is described in terms
of...values. We all have many different values, but
there is only one that we all share—life. Life is the
absolute, universal, and superseding value. In this
complex world of competing relative values, it is
important to understand what values are, as well as,
to be able to differentiate between the different kinds
of values.

We often hear that some people have "good
values" and others have "bad values," but, what does
that really mean? What actually *are* values? What are
good values versus bad values? And how does one

make the distinction? Much of the time we can tell, just by the context, whether a person does something "good" or does something "bad." But, it is not always clear-cut. This is where that word "clarify" comes into play. If we are to live like Ethical Warriors, we must have a clear understanding of what values are in the first place so that we can make sure we possess and practice "good" ones. So what are they?

Here are some common definitions of values compiled by Dictionary.com:

1. "Things that have an intrinsic worth in usefulness or importance to the possessor."
2. "Principles, standards, or qualities considered worthwhile or desirable."
3. "Beliefs people have about what is right and wrong and what is most important in life, which control their behavior."

These seem clear enough. Values can be things, qualities or beliefs that we consider to be...valuable. When considering these definitions of values, we may think of a value as something good. But is that what the definitions really say? Upon close examination, we see that almost all values are really neutral—we might say *amoral*—until we somehow qualify them with questions such as: "How is it good?" or "Good to whom?" When we do that, it becomes clear that the "good" is often purely subjective—just a matter of opinion or taste, or driven by culture, religion, habit, circumstance or the environment. People may "value" vastly different, even conflicting, things. For example, we may "value" a favorite team and see their winning a game as being "good," but couldn't another person view the same outcome as "bad" if he or she "values" the team that lost the game?

There are many examples of values dichotomies. For example, food is good and necessary for life, but we might like some kinds of food and not others. Another person might have a totally different opinion of what kind of food is "good." And if you overeat or eat the wrong kinds of food, food can be bad. We "value" being healthy, but may also strongly "value" the taste of big, fattening donuts. Similarly, drugs can be "good" if they make you well when you're sick, but they can be "bad" if you are a drug abuser and the drugs *make* you sick. People have very different opinions on the nature of such apparent virtues as honor or justice or even truthfulness. This kind of subjective analysis goes on all of the time with many things in life. Ever heard of a love-hate relationship?

It is important to understand that nearly all values are subjective or "relative." They can actually be good and bad, depending on the circumstance, or even one's point of view. Therefore, relative values can be good some of the time and not others—or, good according to some people, but not everyone.

Now that we understand that most values are relative, can you think of a value that is not relative? Does a value exist that everyone can agree on? In a world full of different ethnicities, cultures, religions, nationalities, behavior sets, opinions, likes and dislikes it may be difficult—even controversial—to say that there is even such a thing as a *universal* or *absolute* value. Perhaps the best way to address this point is to relate a true story told by my graduate school professor, Dr. Robert L. Humphrey. This is the first story he told us in that fateful class in San Diego when I was a young Marine. When I think back, I still feel the prickly sensation on the back of the neck that you get when you have an epiphany or life-changing insight. The implications of this story are of clear importance to this day in discussing the concept of mankind's objective, universal value. We call it:

The "Hunting Story"

After his service, during the Cold War, Humphrey took a State Department job overseas. His mission was to stop Anti-American demonstrations at a U.S. missile base in an underdeveloped allied country.

After World War II America was the undisputed leader of the world. For a while it seemed that everyone loved us, even our former enemies. But soon people began to resent us—probably due to our superior attitudes. The term used to describe this attitude was "Ugly Americanism."

We Americans thought that the ingratitude and dislike that many people felt for us was unjustified. After all, we had defeated fascism in World War II and were rebuilding many parts of the world out of our own generosity. Still, the dislike for Americans overseas was real—and growing.

In one particular country, the unrest was beginning to have strategic implications during that delicate time of détente. The trouble centered on the presence of an American missile base there. There were demonstrations outside the gates of the base, burnings of the American flag and some low-level sabotage. Basically, the local people were saying that they wanted the Americans to go home (sound familiar?). Humphrey's job was to find a solution to the conflict—we couldn't just go home.

There were issues from the U.S. point of view as well. Many of the Americans working in that poor allied country didn't like the culture or the relatively austere conditions. Actually it was worse than that. Many saw the local people as "dumb, dirty, dishonest, disloyal, lazy, unsanitary, immoral, violent, cruel, crazy and downright subhuman," and what's worse, they let them know it. No matter what he did, Dr. Humphrey couldn't stop the negative talk— partially because some of it seemed true from an American perspective!

One day, as a diversion, Humphrey went hunting for wild boar with some people from the American embassy. They took an open-backed truck from the motor pool and headed out to the boondocks, stopping at a village to hire some local men to beat the brush and act as guides.

This village was very poor. The huts were made of mud and there was no electricity or running water. The streets were unpaved dirt and the whole village smelled like animal dung. Flies buzzed everywhere. The men looked surly and wore dirty clothes. The women covered their faces, and the children had runny noses and were dressed in rags.

It wasn't long before the talk started in the truck. One American said, "This place stinks." Another said, "These people live just like animals." A third said: "Yeah, they just don't value life the same as we do." Finally, a young air force man said, "They got nothin' to live for; they may as well be dead."

What could you say? It seemed true enough.

But just then, an old sergeant in the truck spoke up. He was the quiet type who never said much. In fact, except for his uniform, he kind of reminded you of one of the tough men in the village. He looked at the young airman and said with a country drawl, "You think they got nothin' to live for, do you? Well, if you are so sure, why don't you just take my knife, jump down off the back of this truck, and go try to kill one of them?"

There was dead silence in the truck.

Humphrey was amazed. It was the first time that anyone had said anything that had actually silenced the negative talk about the local people. The sergeant went on to say, "I don't know either why they value their lives so much. Maybe it's those snotty nosed kids, or the women in the pantaloons. But whatever it is, they care about their lives and the lives of their loved ones, same as we Americans do. And if we don't stop talking bad about them, they're going to kick us out of this country!"

Humphrey then asked the sergeant what we Americans, with all our wealth, could do to prove our belief in the peasants' equality despite their impoverished existence. The sergeant answered easily, "You got to be brave enough to jump off the back of this truck, knee deep in the mud and sheep dung. You got to have the courage to walk through this village with a smile on your face. And when you see the smelliest, scariest looking peasant, you got to be able to look him in the face and let him know, just with your eyes, that you know he is a man who hurts like you do, and hopes like you do, and wants for his kids just like we all do. It is that way or we lose."

This story affects most of us emotionally. We viscerally sympathize with the poor villagers, perhaps because many of us are natural "under-dog" lovers. In America, our own Revolutionary War started because the British looked down on us. A popular cry from that time was, "Don't tread on me." It was even on an early American flag.

According to Humphrey, the point of the story is this: Beneath our culture, beneath the fine clothes or the dirty rags, beneath the color of our skin, we all love life, we all hurt sometimes, and we all want for our children. The people in that village weren't speaking out, but in their hearts each of them was saying: "Don't look down on me. You are my equal— my life, and the lives of my loved ones, are as important to me as yours are to you."

The Americans suddenly understood two things. First, despite how worthless the villagers' lives might appear, no one in that truck would actually try to kill any of them because taking innocent human life is anathema to all moral people. Second, if attacked, the villagers would have defended themselves with all their might because they valued their lives and the lives of their loved ones just as much as anyone else.

This value appears to be a universal value. Humphrey called it the "Life Value." I have been to many places around the world and I have seen it in action everywhere. It makes a simple kind of sense and we need not over-intellectualize this point: we all *must* have this value, or we wouldn't be alive. In fact, when we see or hear of someone who does not want to live or commits suicide, we think that it is very unnatural, that it is wrong, that it is an exception and not the rule. The overwhelming majority of us want to live, and this is our most important value. It is a basic desire felt deeply in the guts of all people everywhere. It is also consistent, it could be said, with the concepts of an "unalienable right to life" and "human equality" found in the U.S. Declaration of Independence. At last, here was Humphrey's way to make the truth that "all men are created equal" truly self evident.

Before we move on, let's get personal with this differentiation between relative values and the objective value of life. Ask yourself: Are there smarter people than you? Better looking? Stronger? Can you accept that? Are some people more educated? Richer? Members of a relatively more highly regarded social class or religion? Are there people who have done more good works in their lives than you have? Are some of a different race, creed or color? Of course! Can you live with all of that? Perhaps so. But what if someone were to say that one or more of those relative differences made the lives of those other people worth more than your life? What would you say? Undoubtedly you would say "No!" Almost all human values and traits can be relative or varying in degrees, but life itself is not. That feeling is shared by all people everywhere—in other words it is universal.

The intrinsic value of Life is a universal *feeling*, but is it real? It sounds reasonable, but is it logical? If we think about it we would, again, have to say "yes."

Logically, life is an absolute and universal value because it is a fundamental requirement of all human existence. Babies come into the world screaming to live. Most people, even in comas, maintain their lives, autonomically and without conscious thought, until the physical machinery wears out. The Life Value is *that* fundamental and that powerful. Life can be expressed as a binary code, 1 or 0, on or off, living or dead. No life, no human existence. Only life has that essential characteristic; no other value has it! It is rarely acknowledged as such, but, as Humphrey happily discovered, it is self-evident, as in the line from the Declaration of Independence that states: "We hold these truths to be self-evident, that all men are created equal, that they are endowed by their Creator with certain unalienable[8] Rights, that among these are Life, Liberty and the pursuit of Happiness." Or if you prefer, as Aristotle said: "A is A."[9]

Some models that attempt to identify the similarities between human beings focus on traits. For example, anthropologist Donald Brown has identified hundreds of traits that humans share, from "abstraction in speech and thought" to "having a world view."[10] Although we do share many traits, those too are relative. Some people are taller or shorter, bigger or smaller, darker or lighter. But they

---

[8] Although Thomas Jefferson used the word "unalienable" in the Declaration of Independence. Inalienable is truer to the word's Latin roots, and while Jefferson's word has always been listed as an accepted variant, inalienable is now the more common form. Both mean incapable of being transferred to another or others.

[9] This is called the "Law of Identity," the earliest use of this principle is thought to appear in Plato's dialogue Theaetetus in 185

[10] Brown, D.E. 1991. Human Universals. New York: McGraw-Hill

are still human beings, aren't they? Genetically, we are all at least 99.5% similar.[11] In fact, it is because of the Life Value that we have any relative diversity of humanity at all. Even a shallow study of human genetic traits leads us back to the universal. Those traits, skin color for example, serve to preserve life. Early in human history, light skinned (low melanin) people would not have thrived in sun-baked equatorial regions. Conversely, dark skinned (high melanin) people living in the northern latitudes with less direct sunlight would have suffered the life-threatening effects of low vitamin D. Both skin tones serve the Life Value; they developed based upon what was life-protecting in a particular environment. But even those differences are relative, and are thought of in a totally separate way than you think about whether someone is alive or not.

Another example is the epicanthic fold that is obvious in the eyes of most people of Asian extraction. The fold evolved to protect the eyes from the extreme sunlight and cold weather of Mongolia, where most Asian people originated.[12]

Back to clarifying: What exactly is the "Life Value?" Is it for real? Do people really believe in it? Is it universal? Are all men and women really created equal? Our observation is that the simple answer is yes. But it is a subtle concept, hard to put into words.

---

[11] For more details, please reference The Council For Responsible Genetics: http://www.councilforresponsiblegenetics.org.

[12] By the way, the epicanthic fold is something that all babies are born with, even non-Asian babies, although those who may not be of Eastern Asian origin will eventually lose the fold.

Simply stated, the intrinsic value of life, whether acknowledged intellectually or not, is universally *felt*. Everybody "feels" that their lives and the lives of their loved ones are as important to them as yours are to you. People understand this concept as the meaning of Human Equality, and they want all others to respect them as equals. People do not like the feeling when others look down on them, or consider them or their group inferior or "sub-human." They (we) do not like the feeling because it is a direct threat to life: If I or my loved ones are considered sub-human then our lives are in jeopardy. Disrespect is a threat to the life value that can be *felt!* Though people all over the world recognize that they may be relatively different from each other in many ways, they also feel that the value of their life is *not* relative. And because life is a requirement of our existence, it is an inalienable right. This is of critical importance in human affairs. Ultimately, most humans won't put up with people who are disrespectful of their lives. It seems to be the same in every culture.

This deep sense of the objective value of life manifests itself in human nature as a feeling of human equality. People everywhere *feel* that the value of their lives is equal to everyone else's—whether they can express it in logical terms or not. The value of life is the great equalizer, even if it is clear that we all may be different in every other—but relatively less important—way. Again, the Life Value, articulated or not, is deeply felt.

Here is the next important point: Because the Life Value feeling is universal, it must go both ways. As we sit in the truck in that remote back-country village, we realize not only that the people on the ground are our equals, but that the people flying overhead, looking down at *us* from their private jets sipping champagne from crystal glasses, are also our equals. Human Equality applies to us, too!

Understanding the nature of values gives us the insight that behavioral, cultural or religious values—that is, what we do to live, or how we live—are relative; but that the Life Value is not. There is a saying attributed to Native Americans that "before we can truly understand another person, we must walk for a time in their moccasins." This seems to support the idea that we are "equal inside," despite our outward differences. As we are all equal, we would pretty much act the same way as those "different" people if we had to live in their environment. At least we could understand why they may act differently.

We will address this subject of a universal Life Value in many ways and from different angles in the pages that follow. For now, as part of our "clarification process," let us work on getting a better understanding of relative values.

Relative values are all values other than the objective value of life. The Life Value is intrinsic, universal and absolute; all other values are clearly not. It bears repeating that relative values are subjective and often represent an opinion or preference. For example, liking vanilla ice cream instead of chocolate, or preferring one football team to another, are relative values because they are held by some people sometimes, but not by all people all the time.

It is also logical that relative values are not necessarily equal—and don't have to be. They can be different from one person or group to the next and still be perfectly valid. Relative values are dynamic, shifting, sometimes confusing and often troublesome, but they are usually not a matter of life or death. Respect for the Life Value often is—look at all the wars and killing going on every day around the world. The lesson of the Hunting Story is that *everyone* believes that their life is equal. So why don't people simply tolerate each other's relative values and respect each other's lives? Shouldn't the fact that we all share the Life Value trump the other differences we have? Where are our priorities? Why doesn't everyone treat everyone else as equals?

People fail to treat each other as equals and with respect for many reasons. One reason is that some relative values are harmful to others—either purposely or by mistake. One other, more subtle, reason seems to be that some relative values can be very connected to—almost inseparable from—the Life Value. If another person doesn't share those values with us it may make us feel that they are ignorant, inferior, or even dangerous. For example, it may seem that preferences in styles of dress are relative. I have my style and you have yours. One style of dress that often causes controversy is the wearing of fur. Some people find the wearing of animal skins or furs to be cruel and unnecessary. But, for someone who lives a nomadic life in the Arctic, a fur coat may be more than just a style preference. In that isolated, life-threateningly cold environment, fur may be the only material available to keep them warm (and alive!). On the other hand, people who live on tropical islands don't wear fur coats, not because they necessarily have an issue with wearing fur for the animals' sake (although they might), but because it is too hot. They could die of heat stroke. They may wear grass skirts — or next to nothing! Others may find *that* style of dress unacceptable according to their relative value system.

Some relative values (favorite ice cream flavors or brands of sneakers, etc.) are a mere matter of personal preference. Certain other relative values, however, may be very necessary for supporting or protecting the Life Value within a particular physical, or even social, environment. Since those particular relative values are necessary to support life, they may attain a status of extreme importance. Therefore we can call them moral values. Moral values protect life.

That seems clear, but it is still not simple. Some relative values can be moral or not — again, depending on the environment or situation. Would it be moral (life protecting) to make your children wear grass skirts in the Arctic Circle? Of course not; they would probably freeze to death. Therefore we can say that the morality of certain relative values can be judged in relationship to the Life Value. In other words, a relative value is moral when it serves to support the absolute value of life (protects life); when the same relative value does not support the Life Value it can be deemed harmful or immoral. Moral values protect/support/respect/honor/sustain the Life Value. Immoral values are immoral because they don't.

That is why moral relativism is illogical. Moral relativism as a concept means that *anything* can be moral; it just depends on the circumstances. We have said that almost all values are relative. *Almost all does not mean all*. Circumstances cannot be the "qualifier" of whether a value or action is moral, because *circumstances change*. They, too, are relative. How can you use a relative value to qualify a relative value? That is illogical. There has to be some *objective* reference point to use as a baseline when evaluating whether a value is moral, doesn't there?

Perhaps an analogy will help. The road to moral behavior is like any other journey in that you must orient yourself before you start. If you want to head west, for instance, how do you know which direction is west? One way is to use the sun. But it has to be daytime and sunny out and you need to know approximately what time it is. Another, more reliable way is to use a compass. But you still need one more thing. You need an immutable point of reference: a true north to calibrate your compass. Only then can you orient yourself and head west.

Trying to navigate a world of relative values with no objective value would be like trying to live in a world where there is no "true north." The needle of your compass would point any old way. You would be apt to wander aimlessly. The same could be said of values. That is why life can be considered the "true north" of the moral compass. Acknowledging the Life Value as your reliable point of reference can help you orient yourself in terms of all the other relative values.

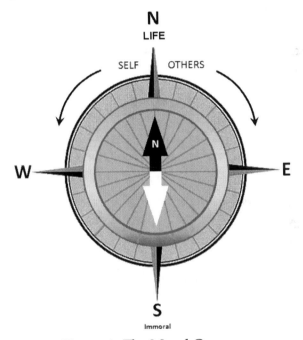

Figure 1- The Moral Compass

Are certain actions good? Good for whom? Should I do this? Or that? Obviously it is impossible to know, or even comprehend, the potential impact of every action you might take on yourself and every other person in the world who may be affected. Would that make our organic ability to keep the balance between self and others imperfect? Probably. But, that does not make life invalid as the primary value and our moral "true north."

Clearly we don't all have perfect value systems. Even people with compasses sometimes go astray or wander. But we do a pretty good job of staying moral most of the time because, as we will continue to explore, it is part of our nature. We can also more reliably do the right thing once we have "calibrated our moral compass." First, we must clarify our starting point: our best effort to balance concern for self and others with life as the "true north." When do we *really* need a compass? When we are lost. What tool would be very useful if we were to be "lost" in a moral gray area? Exactly. A moral compass—and a moral true north.

Most of us don't mean to become lost in a morass of immoral relative values on purpose. But we do, don't we? We humans disrespect—and kill—people all the time. We also hurt and kill ourselves with poor diets, alcohol, drugs, tobacco, lack of exercise, and stress. The values represented by these choices aren't life-protecting. We have the ability to recognize them as such—and do something about them if we want and choose to. Of course, some people practice immoral behavior in order to benefit themselves and harm others. We call them immoral—or criminals.

Moral values can also misfire. Values that are normally life-protecting can somehow become unbalanced and cease serving their original life protecting purpose. As part of my work with the Marine Corps Martial Arts Program I analyzed the Marine Corps core values in this context. It was an interesting—and instructive—exercise. The Marine Corps core values are: Honor, Courage and Commitment. Here are the explanations for these terms that all Marines are taught:

Honor. Honor guides us to exemplify the ultimate in moral behavior; to never lie, cheat or steal; to abide by an uncompromising code of integrity; respect human dignity; and respect others. The qualities of maturity, dedication, trust and dependability commit us to act responsibly; to be accountable for our actions; to fulfill our obligations; and to hold others accountable for their actions.

Courage. Courage is our mental, moral and physical strength. It carries us through the challenges of combat and helps us overcome fear. It is the inner strength that enables us to do what is right; to adhere to a higher standard of personal conduct; and to make tough decisions under stress and pressure.

Commitment. Commitment is the spirit of determination and dedication found in Marines. It leads to the highest order of discipline for individuals and units. It is the ingredient that enables 24-hour a day dedication to Corps and country. It inspires the unrelenting determination to achieve a standard of excellence in every endeavor.

The Marine Corps core values support and clarify the ethos and actions of Marines, and are consistent with the warrior role as protectors and defenders of our constitution, country and Corps. They are great values, don't you think? What could possibly be wrong with them? Nothing is wrong with them...as long as they are tied to the Life Value. Think about it. Without that foundational self-others balance, courage can become foolish martyrdom; commitment can become irrational fanaticism; honor can become self-righteousness, or conceit and disrespect for others. These are what may be called moral value "misfires."

While working on the Ethical Warrior concept I once pointed out to a group of Marines that our enemies have their own standard of honor, they often display great courage, and they are surely committed. I then asked the controversial question: "Does this mean we have the same core values as they do?" It was a show stopper. People didn't know how to respond. The next question was just as important: "Then what sets us apart?" That one was even more difficult to answer. We all felt that there was a difference, but we found that difference hard to articulate. The answer is clear if you think about it: what sets us apart from our enemies is respect for the intrinsic value of *all* life, not just the lives of those in our "in-group." Those who harm and kill innocent men, women and children for a "cause" (consisting of a set of relative values) must be stopped, killed or captured. Why? To stop the killing. Period. When you must *kill to protect life* it is very hard, but it is moral. As paradoxical as that concept may sound at first, it is true. On the other hand, those who would kill anyone not observant of their religious, ethnic or criminal values—in other words, *kill over relative values*—are immoral. Our dedication to protecting all life—rather than just promoting our own relative values—makes us different and ethical.

We must be very careful to keep it that way. To maintain the moral high ground when the enemy acts immorally requires great philosophical discipline and consistency on our part. It would be easy to say that they have done bad things, so we have the right to do bad things back. Or that "our way of life" is better than theirs and justifies immoral behavior (our ends justify the means). But then we would be making the same mistake as they are: rationalizing war and killing based upon our own relative values. Misfire.

Values "misfires" that lead to war and killing are obviously bad. Most people agree that war and killing are awful and should be avoided if at all possible. We certainly want to make sure that we have a clearly moral cause before we participate—or our country participates—in a war. Yet, misfires can happen with any of the values often thought of as "good" when they stop serving the Life Value. For example, hard work can become workaholism (we already mentioned over-eating and improper drug use).

Even the "great" moral values can sometimes misfire. Moral values (some may use the term "virtues") such as charity, compassion, courage, courtesy, creativity, dependability, generosity, honesty, integrity, justice, kindness, love, loyalty, mercy, moderation, patience, perseverance, righteousness, service, sincerity, tact, temperance, thrift, truth, tolerance, wisdom, etc., are all considered great because they are particularly respectful of life. They enhance the life of self, the life of others, or both. But they are all relative.

An example of a great moral value that seems universal is "truth." We would probably say that the truth is the truth and that it is a universally good thing. But what if a murderer was asking you if your children were home so he could go there and kill them? Wouldn't lying better protect life than the "truth?" Those hiding Anne Frank and her family lied to the Nazis, allowing them to survive as long as they did. In that case, lying was moral; telling the truth would have been immoral. If someone had asked me where Anne Frank was hiding, I hope I would have lied, too.

Once at a training session I asked, rhetorically, if truth as a value was relative. Without missing a beat, an experienced police officer said, "Absolutely. I am an undercover agent. When a drug dealer holds a gun to my head and asks if I am a cop, I lie, you bet I lie." The value of Life easily trumps the value of truth.

Another relative moral value that benefits from further examination is one of America's most highly cherished values—freedom. As we have discussed, human equality is a corollary of the Life Value. If we are all equal, it seems to follow that we should also all be free of domination by others. We Americans, particularly, cherish our freedom, because we know that it was won for us with the blood (lives) of our warriors and protectors. Freedom is very close to the Life Value for us, because of that very reason. But freedom is one of those moral values that also require a certain environment for most of us to enjoy it.

Freedom is not an objective value. People often feel the need to balance freedom with security. There is a statement attributed to Benjamin Franklin that "those who would give up Essential Liberty to purchase a little Temporary Safety, deserve neither Liberty nor Safety." Most of us would agree with that—few would willingly give up our essential freedoms. But Mr. Franklin didn't say that we should have *no* safety—a certain amount of security is important. It's a fine line that should be drawn very carefully. Certainly we want freedom, but if there is not enough security (police) in the environment, immoral people are also "free" to practice their criminal, life-threatening behaviors.

A close friend, who trained the Baghdad police after the fall of Saddam Hussein, told the story of a local police chief he was working with during that chaotic time. While grateful for what the Americans had done to facilitate the removal of Hussein from power, the chief was still very irritated by our constant focus on freedom. Finally he complained to my friend, "Please stop talking about freedom. Until my little girl can go to school without being attacked by some insurgent thug, I don't want freedom. I want security."

Who wants freedom if it means that every thug is also "free" to rob or hurt people? Freedom is a relative moral value because it requires the balancing moral value of mutual respect—respect for the Live Value. British philosopher John Stuart Mill wrote in his 1859 essay On Liberty: "The liberty of the individual must be thus far limited; he must not make himself a nuisance to other people." It actually goes way further than that. In the real world, freedom may require active security—a reasonable amount of protection from threats and harm to life. We want freedom, yet no one should be free to falsely yell "fire" in a crowded movie theater. Professor Humphrey explained the balance quite well: "We want as much liberty as *possible,* but as much security as is *necessary.*"

Getting that right balance between freedom and control is very difficult; few people agree on what the exact formula should be. That is why our relative moral values must be constantly balanced by reason and examined and re-examined in relation to the Life Value in order to make sure they are always performing their life-protecting missions. When there is an irresolvable conflict, we humans have learned to utilize the wisdom of objective others—for example, judges or mediators—to make certain that justice prevails.

As we are on the topic of core American values, let's discuss the relativity of the term "the pursuit of happiness." Most people consider this to be an inalienable right and, as such, a great moral value. It proceeds directly from the freedom value. Yet, we can probably agree that notions of happiness are relative; and no one should pursue happiness at the direct expense of another. Immoral people do that. Life as a universal value is primary—all men are created equal; their relative values and behaviors are not.

So we see that the statement: "We hold these truths to be self-evident, that all men are created equal, that they are endowed by their Creator with certain unalienable Rights, that among these are Life, Liberty and the Pursuit of Happiness," can be more fully appreciated when we understand the difference between the Life Value and the great relative values. The American Declaration of Independence contains references to Human Equality and acknowledges both the universal, absolute value of Life, but also the importance of relative moral values.

Life, Liberty and the Pursuit of Happiness are "core" values that are particularly dear to Americans, probably because our revolution was in response to oppression—a relative lack of liberty. Unjust taxation and other practices were actually life-threatening to the American colonists, and they eventually wouldn't put up with it. This feeling is not uniquely American.

All people want their lives to be respected and that means they need to be free from life-threatening controls. It may take time, but people everywhere will resist constraints on vital things that protect and enhance their lives. They will do it peacefully—by consensus or voting—or through protest, rebellion, insurgency or revolution, if there is no other process available to them. You can count on it.

Yet, liberty (or freedom) is a relative value that must be balanced; without adequate protection of life and respect for human equality it is bound to degenerate into chaos, or even worse, tyranny. Count on that, too.

Happiness, of course, seems like a moral value, but it is also relative. What makes one person happy may be different than what pleases another. That relativity is fine, just as long as one person's freedom or happiness does not supersede the Life Value of others—or even himself or herself! Therefore, we should be free to pursue happiness, as long as we do not violate someone else's inalienable right to life. I believe that is what the American Founding Fathers meant. Yet, Gary Wills wrote: "When Jefferson spoke of pursuing happiness, he had nothing vague or private in mind. He meant a public happiness which is measurable; which is, indeed, the test and justification of any government."[13] That sounds as if

---

[13] Gary Wills, Inventing America: Jefferson's Declaration of Independence, Mariner Books (November 14, 2002) Page 164.

happiness is really more connected to the Life Value than to an individual's perspective on his or her own person happiness. What do you think?

Can some cherished relative values be inimical to the Life Value? Perhaps. Some relative values, though not necessarily criminal, may seem just plain wrong—customs that involve dangerous activities, like the indiscriminate firing of weapons, for example, or unsanitary habits, or unsafe motor vehicle operation. So, why do some people still practice them? One reason may be scientific ignorance. Another is because these customs are sometimes, or under certain circumstances, consistent with the Life Value. So there is confusion.

But the philosophical answer is frighteningly simple. The Life Value is so basic, that if it isn't activated we tend to take it for granted—and it is easy to dishonor. Relative values, particularly ones with strong emotional attachments, can be that distracting. When the Life Value isn't the standard by which these relative value choices are judged, immoral behavior can be selfishly rationalized away. Actually, it is worse than that, because "my way is better than your way" can easily become "I am better than you;" and then, "my life is worth more than your life."

Closely related is the point that some relative values become so associated with the Life Value that they become—mistakenly—synonymous. Freedom, as we discussed, is one of those values, a free society can easily become a selfish and unhappy one.

Cultural or religious values that can be moral (life-supporting), but are relative, such as a taboo against eating particular kinds of food or requirements that people wear certain kinds of clothes, etc., can also feel like they should be universal. But those kinds of values are only moral when they protect the Life Value; they can become immoral if they lose the connection with their original, life-supporting purpose.

Can you see how dangerous it can become when relative values supersede the intrinsic value of Life? Think of the Nazis: they viewed Aryan cultural and racial values as superior to the lives of non-Aryans. That allowed them to rationalize that if you were not of their preferred cultural/national/racial group, your life was not considered of value. You were considered sub-human — and could be exterminated.

Unfortunately, what happened in Germany was nothing new. It has happened many times and in many ways through all the ages. It has also happened in America, between different ethnic and racial groups. Sadly, it is still not an antiquated idea — it continues to be a problem all over the world to this day.

When we begin to believe that people who behave in ways that we don't like or agree with have lives that are not as valuable as ours we step on a slippery slope. If an individual's or group's cultural, national, religious values or beliefs are considered sub-par, then the people who practice them, must be sub-par —

or sub-human. If they are not human, then they are not equal. A lack of respect for Human Equality often leads to conflict, then violence, and then killing. Wars often start over a conflict of relative values that, in turn, leads to disrespect for human life.

Remember the massacre of the Tutsis by the Hutus in Rwanda in 1994? It started with resentment between people who were basically neighbors. The conflict began over relative economic values. The Hutus felt that they were at a relative disadvantage to the Tutsi's who enjoyed a greater perceived wealth and social status. The resentment turned into disrespect and demonization. The demonization soon turned into dehumanization (the Hutus began to call their Tutsi neighbors "cockroaches"). Then the dehumanization turned into killing. The dehumanization of the other group was the lethal last step. Can you see how much easier it was to kill a "cockroach" than your neighbor? It was a semantic trick that turned murderous very quickly and with overwhelming power. An estimated 800,000 people were butchered.[14]

Then there was the genocide committed by Bosnian Serb forces of 8,000 Muslims in Srebrenica in 1995. And don't think it can't happen anytime, anywhere. During the Philippine-American War at the turn of the 20th Century, the United States caused the deaths of as many as 250,000 Filipinos (a majority

---

[14] By the way, in order to get a broader perspective, it is important to note that, in 1972, the Tutsi army in Burundi slaughtered between 80,000 and 200,000 Hutus.

of them non-combatants, women and children) until the country was deemed "pacified" by our government on July 4, 1902.

Back at home, Americans were busy "ethnically-cleansing" the continent of Native American Indians. Can you guess the source of the following quote? "The conquest and settlement by the whites of the Indian lands was necessary to the greatness of the race and to the well-being of civilized mankind."[15] How about that for deadly cultural relativism? This sentiment also carried a lot of "official" weight, as the person this quote is attributed to is...President Theodore Roosevelt. (He said a lot of good things, too, but that sentiment was a stinker).

On these cool, rational pages, it seems ridiculous to automatically equate the *way* a person lives (his relative values) with the value of his life. It is easy to see that these two types of values are fundamentally different and should not be confused. But, in reality, it is very easy to judge other people by their relative values (how they act or look), particularly if the values of "those others" are strange, different, hard to understand, or seem illogical or threatening to us.

We will further explore this topic in the book, but, here is the cardinal rule: the Life Value trumps all relative values.

For those who have children, the fallacy of trying to equate relative values with the Life Value is a little

---

[15] Dyer, Thomas G. Theodore Roosevelt and the Ideas of Race, pp 78.

easier to illustrate. Children (especially teenagers!) have behaviors and values that parents like sometimes and thoroughly *dis*like at other times—possibly at the same moment. But we don't consider our children human only when they act in ways that we like and sub-human when they do things we don't like. No, we can easily differentiate the value of their life from the relative value of their behavior. We respect the inalienable value of their life—and love them—regardless of their behavior.

Why wouldn't that logic carry through for people who are not our children? It would seem reasonable that it should. But, we humans are small group animals with millions of years of tribalism in our history. In general, the farther from our own in-group another person or group is, the easier it is to disrespect their life and judge them by their relative values—especially if they have relative values that we don't necessarily like or understand. For millennia, our small group efficacies and loyalties, though relative, were very life-protecting, even life-enhancing. It was *safer* to exclude outsiders or treat them with suspicion, if not outright disrespect, including demonization and dehumanization. Outsiders were often raiders, or competitors for scarce natural resources, such as water and game. But then is not now. In this shrinking world, it is extremely important to keep the fact of human equality in mind and use our powers of reason to overcome the predilection for negative stereotyping and prejudice. It is time to open the circle and let others in.

There are, of course, certain relative behaviors that *are* life-threatening, and we don't have to respect them. That would be cultural relativism. Cultural relativism says that all cultural behaviors are equal, just different, and it is proper to respect them all. That isn't necessary true, at least for every cultural value. Some can be deadly! In fact, one of the jobs of the Ethical Warrior is to stop—perhaps capture or kill—people who practice life-threatening relative values. But, that doesn't mean that we are killing these individuals because they are sub-human or because their life has no value. We stand up to them in order to save life, because all life is to be respected, and the behavior of immoral people can sometimes be life-threatening to others and must be halted.

We will cover this point more thoroughly as we proceed, but let us be clear in saying that when a relative value doesn't support the Life Value it can easily lead to a dangerous and slippery slide into immorality. When *life* is the objective standard by which relative values are judged, we see that certain relative values, even the so called "great moral values," can actually be immoral in certain contexts and cannot be rationalized. The same goes for some of our cherished cultural and behavioral values.

Moral relativists would argue (if they thought in these terms) that respect for "others" means "some others"—those that they would deem worthy. This is dangerous and wrong. But this mistake can be avoided. By using the Life Value as a qualifying value, it becomes clear that respect for the lives of "some others" must reasonably be "all others." This is consistent, I believe, with the "unalienable right to life" and "human equality" concepts found conspicuously in the Declaration of Independence.

We have covered a lot of ground already. Let's recap:

- What are values? Values are "things that have an intrinsic worth in usefulness or importance to the possessor." They can also be "principles, standards, or qualities considered worthwhile or desirable."
- What kinds of values are there? There are basically two kinds of values: (1) The Life Value (a universal and absolute value shared by everyone), and (2) relative values (subjective values that are shared by some people sometimes).
- What is the Life Value? It is the intrinsic value of life. The American 1776 value "all men are created equal" is an acknowledgement that Life is an intrinsic value shared by all people. Life is also a absolute value because life is fundamental to human existence. If we didn't

have it, we wouldn't be alive. No other value has that characteristic.

- What are relative values? Relative values are all other values beside the Life Value. Relative values can reflect a matter of taste, opinion or belief, or depend on the specific environment in which they are practiced. Relative values are subjective and inherently amoral until qualified by the Life Value.
- What are moral values? Moral values are relative values that protect, sustain, respect, protect, and/or honor the Life Value.
- Are the great moral values absolute? No, they are relative. They must be *qualified* by the Life Value to be considered moral. But they certainly are great when they are performing their life-respecting mission.

We have discussed two things with regard to the Life Value: that the equal value of our lives is a feeling we all have, and that it is also reasonable—we all have the Life Value, or we wouldn't be alive. It is just that fundamental, and I recommend, at least for now, that you don't over-think that point.

It is time for us to delve deeper into the other side of the Life Value. That is the side that pertains to, not only ourselves, but to others. Let's discuss life as a *dual* value.

Chapter 3
Self and Others

"The first step in the evolution of ethics is a sense of
solidarity with other human beings."
- *Albert Schweitzer*

"We must treat others as we wish others to treat us."
- *The Golden Rule*

"The relationship between ethics and morals is like
that between theory and practice, since the former
denotes the theory of right conduct and the good life,
whereas the latter refers to the actual practice of right
conduct and the good life."
- *William Sahakian*

Did you notice the exact words that the old
Sergeant used in the Hunting Story? He said: "I don't
know either why they value their lives so much.
Maybe it's those snotty nosed kids, or the women in
the pantaloons." That is an important clue to a further
understanding of the full scope of the Life Value.
When we talk about the Life Value, whose life,
exactly, are we talking about?

If we were to state the obvious, we would say that
life is a dual value: ourselves and at least some others.
Before we examine more closely *which* others are

included in that statement, we might first ask: Is the Life Value a predominantly selfish one? One often hears the quote, usually attributed to Samuel Butler, that, "self preservation is the first law of nature." Is that really true? Here is a surprising Robert Humphrey story from the battle of Iwo Jima that sheds light on this question. It is the second story that he used in that California university classroom to slowly and gently guide his students toward a deeper understanding of human nature. As you read, ask yourself this: if you were the young platoon leader, would *you* think that life was a selfish value?

The "Volunteer"

On the sixth day of the battle for Iwo Jima, I [Humphrey] took command of the only six (teenage) American Marines who were still left in a front-line rifle platoon that had more than 40 original members [Company F/2/28].

After losing his closest friends during those first six days, the evening that I took command, a young Marine named Mercer told me, skeptically, that I was their sixth lieutenant in those six days. Then, as he "dug in" for the night, he suddenly started denouncing the top cultural values that had been instilled in us Marines during that age of high patriotism. "Fuck the Marine

Corps![16]" He shouted. "Fuck democracy and
fuck this war! I don't volunteer for nothing. I
DON'T VOLUNTEER FOR NOTHING!"
Four of the other five Marines took up that
chant. "Right," they yelled, "I don't volunteer
for nothing! I don't volunteer for nothing."

As their new leader, I knew I had been
warned (I was just 22-years-old myself.) The
first thing the next morning, an order came in
for me to send a "volunteer" straight out
front on an extremely dangerous, almost
certain-death, reconnaissance mission.
Thinking about that chant and feeling fresh,
compared to those exhausted, young combat-
veterans who had already shot their way
across the base and up to the top of Mt.
Suribachi (during the patrol before the
famous flag-raising), I decided to go myself
rather than appoint an enlisted "volunteer."

As I started to crawl forward in the
detestable black sand, Mercer, knowing that
it was foolish leadership for me, the officer,
to go, crawled over into my face, blocking my
path, and said, authoritatively: "My turn, I'll
go." I was taken aback. "Weren't you the guy
who said last night that you don't volunteer
for nothing?" "Well, Lieutenant," he said, "I

---

[16] If seeing that word in print shocks you...try to imagine the shock that Humphrey felt
hearing that vulgarity referring to the fanatically revered Marine Corps...from an armed,
agitated, and aggressive man in a war zone.

can't trust a shavetail[17] like you on a mission like this." Stunned, I realized what Mercer was really saying: "My turn to die, Lieutenant—not yours." [18]

According to Humphrey, the irreducible facts of human survival are clear: the best men voluntarily do the dying, if necessary, to save the group whose members are less morally and/or physically capable. Humphrey found that as the fatalities mounted in a platoon, the men began to question and denounce the cultural values that they were being asked to die for: honor, country, democracy, the Marine Corps, etc. *But they virtually never failed to protect each other.*

There are some nuances to this; in personal correspondence Humphrey continues:

Human nature as I saw it on Iwo Jima is not such that everyone acts heroically. But human nature *is* such that the best of us humans do act heroically to save the group. Actually, it is even more sophisticated than that. When "the "best" is killed while trying to protect a group, the next best fighters tend to recognize that they are now "the most capable." Sometimes this assumption of leadership continues right on down the line to those who are the weakest, and they too

---

[17] Shavetail is an "affectionate" term for an inexperienced young officer.
[18] George Mercer was wounded in action and later killed during the last days of the fight when his hospital tent was overrun. He received a Navy Cross posthumously.

will step forward toward that horror of possible death when other lives in their "in-groups" are threatened. The "in-group" feeling is a trigger, but I found in my later conflict resolution work that the "in-group" feeling is not hard to expand even across the historic barriers of ethnic hatreds spawned from bloodletting.

This story illustrates that the Life Value is a dual value—self *and others*. Terrence Des Press discusses similar observations in his book on the Nazi prison camps. He said "the best of us did not live...the best gave their lives so others could."[19]

Figure 2 – Balanced Life Value

The most subtle lesson in that Iwo Jima story is that Mercer had very loudly denounced all of his top,

---

[19] Des Press, T., The Survivor: An Anatomy of Life in the Death Camps. Oxford University Press, 1976

culturally instilled (learned or conditioned) values; in other words, his relative values. Those denunciations included rejection of the Marine Corps (that shocked Humphrey the most). But when that self-giving Life Value stood in his face, even though it promised him almost certain death, Mercer, like so many others of "the best," volunteered spontaneously and without dramatics of any kind. It was as if he were merely volunteering to take his turn to "get the coffee." As we have already said, the Golden Rule doesn't seem to address the fact that many of us—in fact, the people we consider the "best"—go above and beyond the Rule.

The Life Value works subtly, but it is clear that "others" has a slight edge over "self." Humphrey's observation seems to reflect this nuance. He often would say, based upon his many years of experience, that the way you can get yourself into the second most danger of all possible ways, everywhere in the world with most persons in the world, is to threaten their lives. If that is the second most dangerous, what is the *most* dangerous thing you can do in the face of those same persons? That's right, threaten their loved ones (their in-group).

Now this, too, seems self-evident. Mothers will protect their children; the captain is the last to leave a sinking ship; a Marine will smother a grenade with his body to protect his buddies, etc. Firefighters rush into burning buildings almost every day to save complete strangers. You can probably think of someone for whom you would risk and, if necessary, give your life. So, why do we also hear people say things like, "self-preservation is the first law of nature?" Obviously, that can't be right.

It is *not* right, but it is close…almost a tie between our "self preserving" and "species preserving" inclinations. Therein lays the confusion. On one hand we seem like self-preservers. One can easily think of a time when a person—even oneself—acted completely, and maybe even criminally, selfish. In another situation that same person might act in the exact opposite way—that is, with amazing unselfishness.

So what is the rule? Is there a rule? Which side *logically* is primary? Self or others? The answer is: It depends. Would you protect your own life? Yes. Are there times when you would risk your life to protect someone else? Yes. When a ship sinks, would it be correct to yell "every man for himself?" Could be. How about, "women and children first?" Also, could be. So, which side of the duality is stronger? Which action is more correct?

If we had a time machine, we could figure it out scientifically. Sink the ship, yell "every man for himself," and count how many people make it to the desert island and live. Then, rewind the scenario and sink the ship again, but this time yell "women and children first." Count how many people survive this time. If the Life Value is the primary value, and all lives are equal, then whichever scenario results in the most lives preserved is the correct answer.

This is impossible, of course; this kind of decision has to be made on the fly and there is no replay. There are always two sides to a values decision—self and others—and we have to make our own best judgment. Changing circumstances could also make the choice very fluid—back and forth between self and others. Tough stuff, but we humans do it remarkably well most of the time.

But, when it becomes a matter of life and death, as a rule, we humans value the ethic: "women and children first," over the ethic: "every man for himself." Think about it, what do we call people who save themselves? We call them survivors. What do we call people who make sure the less capable people are in the lifeboat before thinking to save themselves? We call them heroes, don't we? This reflects a common acknowledgement that we all generally cherish those people who serve others over self. You may have heard a qualifying statement to the effect that "I should protect myself first, or how could I be capable of helping others?" But many of our most cherished heroes did *not* do that. They *sacrificed* themselves for others.

The dual-nature of the Life Value, with its slight tilt toward others in times of trouble, is well recognized in all cultures. Isn't it true that virtually all of us admire those who protect others, especially at the risk of their own lives?

The willingness of human beings to give their lives for others expresses a deep self-giving/species-preserving drive. Self-preservation is a powerful law of nature, but protecting others (especially—but not exclusively—loved ones) is even stronger.

An "interesting" terrorist strategy actually relies on this human proclivity to protect others. The insurgents place two bombs in a crowded area and only set off one. Once people (including not only professional first-responders but other Good Samaritans) rush to the scene to help the victims of that first explosion, the terrorists then set off the second explosion timed to kill the maximum number of innocents. That is just plain evil.

Species-preservation may be an intrinsic drive, but it is also motivated by human nature's strongest rewards: feelings of maturity, wisdom, serenity and incomparable nobility. This feeling of nobility, which life-saving alone provides, is the highest reward for the Ethical Warrior.

During Humphrey's night-and-day experiences of combat on Iwo Jima, which he called a "laboratory of human behavior," this basic, species-preserving value gradually revealed itself to the exclusion of all else. Impending death strips away all the other values that are often cited too casually as "more important than life itself." The extremely high incidence of bravery by the men on behalf of their fellow Marines seemed to indicate that the "protecting others" inclination was strong—stronger even than the fear of one's own death.

Does that mean that we are all potential heroes? Yes and no. It is clear that such factors as innate personal characteristics, level of battle fatigue, possibility of successfully saving others in a particular circumstance, etc., all contribute to whether a person can step up and be an effective "others protector" in combat. However, Humphrey noted that even men who seemed ineffective in combat (not cowards—just too stressed out to function) might become effective if the situation changed such that they found themselves to be the most competent man left (because others were killed or wounded) and had to step up to protect the others. Here is another interesting story from Humphrey's time on Iwo Jima.

Protecting Others on Iwo Jima

In my [Humphrey's] rifle platoon, two of the teenage Marines had "stressed-out" after 34 of their 40 man platoon had been shot in the first five days. Two of the young replacement Marines had also started to stress-out and were neither watching out front for the enemy nor shooting. This was at night when infiltrators were occasionally trying to crawl in on us from out of caves and tunnels nearby seeking food and water.

That next morning, I was raging at them, threatening a court-martial, et cetera, if they did not start shooting to at least protect their own lives. They ignored my entreaties.

A young Texan from near Houston, Clyde Jackson, called softly to me: "You are telling them the wrong thing, Lieutenant. Tell them if they don't start shooting, they will let us others get killed."

That worked. It actually pulled them out of their stress-induced apathy (shell-shock) where the appeal to save their own lives had not.

After Jackson pointed this out to me, I then started using it successfully in other cases. Apparently, when men possess both their wits and the competency to cope with a death-threatening emergency, then a "species-preserving tendency" works like a natural duty. It clearly seemed to be the strongest of all our drives—stronger even than self-preservation.

Still, this topic is much nuanced. There have not been very many battles like Iwo Jima in recorded history. Therefore, there have been few opportunities to study the actions of men who are subjected to close-up killing for such a prolonged period of time that all of their relative values have been stripped away. This is a good thing, of course, but it also makes it difficult to observe and understand the subtleties of human nature at its most elemental level.

This others-protecting type of behavior was not only evident on Iwo Jima, however, it has *often* been apparent in times of great danger when others are at risk. The following Medal of Honor citation is from an incident that occurred in Iraq:

Dunham, Jason L.,
Corporal, United States Marine Corps

For conspicuous gallantry and intrepidity at the risk of his life above and beyond the call of duty while serving as Rifle Squad Leader, 4th Platoon, Company K, Third Battalion, Seventh Marines (Reinforced), Regimental Combat Team 7, First Marine Division (Reinforced), on 14 April 2004.

Corporal Dunham's squad was conducting a reconnaissance mission in the town of Karabilah, Iraq, when they heard rocket-propelled grenade and small arms fire erupt approximately two kilometers to the west. Corporal Dunham led his Combined Anti-Armor Team towards the engagement to provide fire support to their Battalion Commander's convoy, which had been ambushed as it was traveling to Camp Husaybah. As Corporal Dunham and his Marines advanced, they quickly began to receive enemy fire. Corporal Dunham ordered his squad to dismount their vehicles and led one of his fire teams on foot several blocks south of the ambushed convoy. Discovering seven Iraqi vehicles in a column attempting to depart, Corporal Dunham and his team stopped the vehicles to search them for weapons. As they approached the vehicles, an insurgent leaped out and attacked Corporal Dunham. Corporal Dunham wrestled the insurgent to the ground and in the ensuing struggle saw the insurgent release a grenade. Corporal Dunham immediately alerted his fellow Marines to the threat. Aware of the imminent danger and without hesitation, Corporal Dunham covered the grenade with his helmet and body, bearing the brunt of the explosion and shielding his Marines from the blast. In an ultimate and selfless act of bravery in which he was mortally wounded, he saved the lives of at least two fellow Marines. By his undaunted courage, intrepid fighting spirit, and unwavering devotion to duty, Corporal Dunham gallantly gave his life for his country, thereby reflecting great credit upon himself and upholding the highest traditions of the Marine Corps and the United States Naval Service.

Do you think that Corporal Dunham was awarded the Medal of Honor because he "wrestled the insurgent to the ground" to protect himself? Or was it because he "covered the grenade with his helmet and body, bearing the brunt of the explosion and shielding his Marines from the blast?" Easy answer. He was awarded the medal for his actions in defense of the *others*.

The heroic case of Corporal Dunham is clear-cut. But the self/others balance plays itself out in less obvious ways, every minute, every day, in every circumstance. It is *always* operating. As we navigate through life we see that we live a constant balancing act between self and others. Should I be sacrificing for someone else right now? Can I be a little selfish right now? We may not always think of it in those terms, but that's life!

We reward exceptional feats of heroism because they exemplify that "others" protecting inclination that appears to be dominant in human beings, yet, can also be very hard to follow. It is particularly difficult for most of us to keep that balance when we are under stress. It also sometimes becomes harder when the "other" is a person outside of our family, friends and in-group. Clearly it is easier to sacrifice for our own "flesh and blood" than for some nameless outsider, especially if we have time to think about it. A story that illustrates the self and others—all others—paradox is the one about two buildings burning at the same time. One building has 100 people in it and the other building has 50 people in it. You only have one fire truck. Which building do you drive to? Answer: the one with your mother in it.

A scenario like this is clearly a conundrum, but we can probably acknowledge two things: (1) Saving 100 people is a better choice than saving 50 people. But, (2) making the right decision is not always easy and could require sacrifice. We just have to do our best in a situation like this and make our own best judgment.

I contend that we make best judgments when the
Life Value is the starting point and the value of all
lives is acknowledged as fundamentally equal. As
painful as it may be, the default has to be the 100
person building. And you probably would want it
that way, because on another day in another fire, you
or one of your loved ones might actually be in that
larger building. Making the right choice is not always
easy. But, please consider the following true story. It
was witnessed by the great science fiction writer
Robert Heinlein during his childhood; and he told it
during a graduation address at his alma mater, the
U.S. Naval Academy.

The Hobo

One day while strolling through the great
park in Kansas City, he and his mother saw a
young woman get her foot caught in the
tracks at a railroad crossing. The woman's
husband was desperately trying to free her
because a train was bearing down on them.
The train was travelling far too quickly to
stop before the crossing.

As Heinlein and his mother watched the
terrifying situation unfold, a hobo suddenly
appeared and immediately joined the
husband's futile effort to pull the woman
free. But tug and twist as they might, they
could not get her foot unstuck.

The train killed all three of them.

In his description of the vagabond's effort Heinlein observed that the hobo did not so much as look up to consider his own escape. Clearly, it was his intention either to save the woman or to die trying. Heinlein concluded his account of the nameless hero's action with this comment: "This is the way a man dies," but he then added, "And this is the way a man lives."

Humphrey always asked his audiences: What did Heinlein mean when he said, "This is the way a man lives?" After all, he died!

Audiences could seldom fully explain their feelings, but they always realized that the story held meaning for all of our lives. Guided discussion usually revealed that most people thought a noble and generous life was better than a selfish, although possibly longer, one. What do you think?

We have said that all lives are equal. Is it possible to argue that some people's lives are more "valuable" in some ways than others? For example, we might be tempted to say that the hobo's life was really not that valuable—what did he have to lose? Or we might want to say that the life of a general is more important than the life of a private, or that the life of the president is more important than the life of a street sweeper. We might point out that when we yell "woman and children first" on a sinking ship, we should make an exception for a doctor—even if he is a man. In all of these cases there may be people who have certain skills that would ultimately help sustain, protect, or save more lives than some other people. And that may be true, and it may play into our decision-making in times of emergency. Again, we have to make our own best judgments, and we are equipped to do that.

But even special skills don't exempt us from the rule of human equality. The skills may be relatively more valuable, but how about the lives themselves? When you read the first Humphrey Iwo Jima story, did you think that Mercer volunteered because Humphrey was a fellow Marine? On the contrary, Marine or not, Humphrey was an outsider—and, as the "new guy," he was not considered "valuable;" actually, he was probably considered a danger to everyone left in that platoon due to his inexperience. Mercer volunteered for that dangerous mission, and to die if necessary, because he was the *most capable*.

Philosophical and religious documents abound with admonitions to sacrifice for others, and that seems to be consistent with our human nature. Virtually every religion has a version of the "Golden Rule" in its doctrine. Concepts such as charity, respect, humility and kindness are respected and encouraged in most cultures. There may also be biological reasons, totally beneath conscious thought, working behind the scenes that prod us to show genuine concern for others—a "species-preserving" inclination. The fascinating sciences of biology and sociobiology contend that we have an evolutionary or genetic predisposition to pass on our biological material. In terms of the "others" half of the Life Value, this would seem to imply that people will sacrifice for others, but most strongly for those who are in their genetic downstream. This is understandable, perhaps, considering our tribal beginnings, but the ability to make reasonable self-others choices based upon the reality of the way the world is *now* is critical to human well-being today. We are not ants, driven by an instinctive, self-sacrificing loyalty to our colonies alone. Anthropologist and scientist E. O. Wilson said that, although "hard-core" altruism or "kin-based" sacrifice is strong in humans, it is also "the enemy of civilization."[20] It limits our ability to expand our social community outside of our close genetic relatives and limits desirable genetic diversity and cultural evolution. Therefore, our strong, relative in-group favoring inclinations must be balanced by reason.

We may debate whether sacrificing for those outside our "in-group" is a cultural, biological or moral imperative. Regardless, it is certainly reasonable to believe that a diverse and vibrant environment in which to build relationships with genetic "others" is desirable. This pool of others necessarily includes those outside our biological,

---

[20] Wilson, Edward O. On Human Nature. Pp 156.

cultural and social in-groups. Diversity is, ultimately, a good thing. Consider that incest is dangerous to the long-term health and viability of the species, and, as such, represents a taboo almost everywhere. Inbreeding may be practiced in some cultures, but it is the exception and not necessarily desirable. Some cultural values, such as those that promote parochialism, tribalism nepotism, etc., are often *not* good and a little cultural detective work will usually reveal that they are Life Value misfires.

People have been cooperating since the dawn of man. Why? One reason is that, when we cooperate, we increase the survivability of all the individuals in the group, as well as the group itself. Certainly, parents sacrifice to provide for their children. They have to, at least until the children are grown old enough to take care of themselves. Families and groups, for the most part, can and do protect and nurture individuals better than they could themselves. This is all common knowledge. We clearly are a species that protects at least "some others" over self, particularly in times of need. We also do it in times of plenty. But is it just *quid pro quo*? I will help you hunt because it takes a group of us to bring down a stampeding buffalo. We can also share the food before it goes bad. And if I break my leg, you will carry me back to the cave and feed me so I don't starve—and vice versa. So, is it only reciprocal altruism—a matter of efficiency or economics? No, it is more. People *like* to cooperate. It *feels* good. There is a social urge to care for others and it is not only self-serving reciprocal altruism.

The concept of reciprocal altruism, as well as the opposite—that true moral behavior requires that there be *no* material or psychological reward—and all the variant theories in between are well-covered in the literature, so I won't go into them here. What I would say is that it doesn't matter the motivation—it is fine to protect/respect others in any regard. You can enjoy positive feedback from someone that you did something nice for; you can enjoy a good feeling that you got inside for doing something nice for someone who never knew it was you who did it, etc. These are all fine, I think. But I believe that these are "nurture-side" reinforcements of something that is already hard-wired in humans. What I mean by that is, species-preserving proclivities are ingrained in our human nature; we know it, so we encourage ourselves and others to act that way. Nurture.

But consider this: we once interviewed a combat Marine who jumped on a grenade that didn't explode. We asked him what he was thinking before he jumped on the grenade, and he said he didn't think or feel anything; he just did it. That led Humphrey and me to believe that this others' protecting proclivity is hard-wired. Nature. Although, it may be stronger in some of us than others, and stronger under certain circumstances than others, it's human nature. What do you think?

There is much scientific study presently analyzing human biology, chemistry, physiology and even brain waves. Current work being done using MRIs of brain scans provides evidence that preference for fairness activates reward circuitry in the brain.[21] We may soon know—if we don't already—what chemicals make us feel happy and cooperative and how they work. But in terms of values the point is clear. We are preservers, protectors and sustainers of life. That Life Value is a dual value—self and others. All others.

When we look at a list of the great values, we see that they all serve the Dual Life Value of self and others. Some serve the "self-side" such as food, health, beauty, music, serenity, etc. Some serve the "others-side," such as love, charity, truth, faithfulness to others (like the Marine Corps motto *Semper Fidelis*) and the Marine core values of honor, courage and commitment. Some serve both.

It is an elegant and dynamic system. For a normally functioning person in a reasonable environment, the balance between self and species preservation is accomplished organically; that is, it comes naturally from the inside-out. Laws and social mores only codify and reinforce this internal balancing act. There may be biological proclivities— or even philosophical, religious or cultural values-- that are at risk for a "misfire," but these can all be

---

[21] Tabibnia, G., Satpute, A.B., & Lieberman, M.D. (2008). "The sunny side of fairness: Fairness preference activates reward regions (and disregarding unfairness activates self-control circuitry)." Psychological Science, 19:4, 339-347.

countered by reason and self-control. That is the moral imperative. We constantly seek the formula (and, again, it is dynamic) that will best balance the Life Value of self and others.

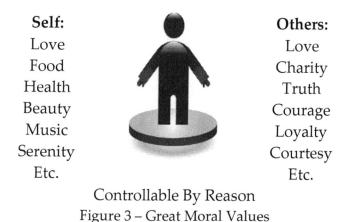

Self:		Others:
Love		Love
Food		Charity
Health		Truth
Beauty		Courage
Music		Loyalty
Serenity		Courtesy
Etc.		Etc.

Controllable By Reason

Figure 3 – Great Moral Values

It is important to highlight the fact that, although people may receive guidance from their culture, religion, governments, other social sources and from each other individually—and even from their genes— it is up to the *individual* to make the right choice, to strike the right balance. We can definitely use the outside help, but human nature is not a "blank slate;" the ability to balance the well-being of self and others is in all of us. Professor Paul Bloom, a psychologist at Yale University in Connecticut, has studied morality in babies for years. He has said that: "A growing body of evidence…suggests that humans do have a rudimentary moral sense from the very start of life.

With the help of well-designed experiments, you can see glimmers of moral thought, moral judgment and moral feeling even in the first year of life. Some sense of good and evil seems to be bred in the bone."[22]

Perhaps you have seen the ubiquitous video of a herd of water buffalo protecting a baby from a pride of lions.[23] It is quite astounding how they fight off the much more physically endowed lions (while also being threatened by crocodiles) to protect one of their own. It would be embarrassing—even shameful—to consider that water buffalo might have this natural others-protecting tendency but humans don't.

It is, in reality, quite dangerous for us to overlook or discount the natural moral sense that is in virtually all of us. If human beings had no *intrinsic* Life Value, wouldn't we have to be "infused" or "imbued" with one from *somewhere* or risk becoming extinct? That moral sense (wherever it came from) would necessarily have to be based upon a dual system of self and others—after all, "no man is an island." And the system would have to be skewed toward protecting others—or what would happen to helpless children, etal? That all begs the question: why trust that the "others-protecting" side will somehow be favored? Why not just create a system that *ensures* that it happens? In actuality, there is such a system. It

---

[22] Bloom, P. (May 2010). The Moral Life of Babies. The New York Times Magazine.
[23] This video is worth watching if you haven't seen it:
http://www.vidmax.com/video/3005/Water_buffalo_versus_lions_versus_the_croc_A
MAZING_VIDEO_/

is called collectivism, a systematic sacrificing of the individual for the group. One might ask why someone didn't anticipate the horrors that would result from forced collectivism *a la* Marxism and Communism. The answer, I think, is understandable, and it derives from the seductive, but deadly philosophical theory of *tabula rasa* or the "blank slate" hypothesis of human nature. *Tabula rasa* means that humans at birth have no intrinsic mental or moral content and virtually all of their knowledge comes from experience and perception. In other words, it presupposes that the Life Value is *not* a universal of human nature, and that individuals have to be "nurtured" into proper human values.

The question then becomes: Which are the proper human values? As we have seen (and the collectivists had it right to this extent), they break down into one of two kinds: those that are of value to the self, and those that are of value to others. What follows is one of the greatest examples of logical disconnect in the history of man. It goes something like this: It is self evident that humans are happier and the species more successful when "others-protecting" values are superior to the "self-protecting" values. Therefore, we should create social, economic and political systems that reflect that "natural" skew toward others. Wait a minute! If a skew toward others is "natural" and "self-evident," why do we need to enforce it? Certainly, the Dual Life Balance can misfire—with people occasionally becoming too selfish or too selfless. We can have controls upon our natural, organic balancing capability that would apply when the balance becomes so off kilter that it is life threatening to self or others. But where did this "self evident" proclivity come from? I would argue that it is natural and embedded in our human nature as a universal and intrinsic Life Value.

Clearly, the opposite can happen as well. If a social system were to reinforce only the selfish values (usually as an over-reaction to collectivism), you end up out of balance the other way. And that "survival of the fittest society" is not utopia, although a lot of "anarchists" might disagree. It is chaos. If you think anarchy is utopia, study what life is like in Mogadishu, Somalia in the early 21st century. Consider what that must be like and let me know if I am wrong.

Human nature is not *tabula rasa*, anyone with two kids, even twins, knows that. If people's character is *only* a result of environmental factors, our kids would all act the same. That's a laugh. But most importantly, we can't just automatically default our society toward "others." That would be neither balanced nor natural. And in such an "others-skewed" society, what do you do with those who can't or won't self-sacrifice every time "the state" tells them to? They must be defective, right? So we must nurture those "selfish" people…in re-education camps, gulags and, if those don't work, killing fields. That's what happened, and that is what will happen again if we don't take care.

A mandated "others" or species-preserving system may sound reasonable, but it negates our need to find the self-others balance on our own. It also leaves the door open for sociopathic, immoral people to manipulate the system for their own benefit. And they do: Observe the behavior of Stalin, Pol Pot, Mao Zedong, etal. They realized that people would be inclined to accept a system that appeared at first exposure to be benignly "unselfish" and structured to protect all of society. They established it—by force— and then maintained it for their own ends and for the benefit of their relative circle of supporters. Horrible.

It would be true to say that all forms of systematic control that supersedes an individual's right to strike his or her own balanced regard for self and others are at risk of becoming abusive. If people become unable to keep the balance (criminals, for example), we are certainly capable of identifying the immoral behavior and addressing those exceptions through sensible civil and legal remedies without making human sacrifice the default. But, ultimately, people will always seek a reasonable balance between self and others. However, if we are not ethical from the inside out, expect our neighbors to demand controls on our behavior from the outside in. If we believe there are too many rules, laws and regulations imposed upon us today, and want fewer of them, then we know what we have to do…

How do we, as a civilization, walk the fine line between anarchy (too much freedom) and collectivism, despotism and the like (too much control)? The answer is simple but difficult. Except for obvious exceptions (murder, rape, stealing, etc.), we have to let it happen naturally. Individual *people* have to seek balance and all of their daily individual "self or others" decisions—some good, some not so good—extrapolate to the whole. It is a little like a bowling alley: you have a gutter on the left side to catch people who are too selfish; and a gutter on the right for people who are too selfless. Leave everybody who stays in the lane alone.

But that is not the trend. Nowadays there seems to be a need for so many laws, rules and regulations that no one can keep up with them. What is the problem? Again, it may be that we, individually, must take greater personal responsibility—become more ethical from the inside out. But then there is the issue of competing relative values, particularly when one set of values is immoral. This clash of values has to be addressed. Clearly, we have criminals who violate the Life Value, and we have laws to address their behavior. We also have civil remedies for disputes between competing relative values. But our human nature constantly impels us to seek our own view of what is balanced, what is right. The trouble is that we sometimes are over-optimistic about our own ability to get a fair balance, and are often suspect of the *other* person's ability to do so, particularly if their behavior impacts us in ways that we don't like. We want to make sure he or she does keep the balance—or make sure someone makes sure they do.

So we have conflict. From a values standpoint, conflict can be defined as competition between values. There are four basic types of conflict:

1. Conflicts between relative values.
2. Conflicts between competing relative values.
3. Conflicts between relative values and the Life Value.
4. Conflicts between Life Values.

When relative values conflict, two things can happen. The first is that we can adopt the approach of "live and let live." I like vanilla, you like chocolate. You practice Islam, I practice Catholicism, and she practices Buddhism. And we leave it at that. I respect your choice (even though I don't share your value), and you do the same. These kinds of conflicts do not have to be resolved.

When relative values clash, however, we have a second type of situation, one that we have to work out. Let us say we are out to buy ice cream and we can only buy one flavor. Which flavor will it be? We can adopt the approach of "give and take." We resolve it based upon the relative strength of our "ice cream values." Maybe you don't care so much or I don't. Maybe we base our decision on precedent—we had your favorite last time, we'll have mine this time. Maybe we don't buy any, because that is the fairest way to keep the balance. We resolve the conflict amiably.

As we know, there are two basic kinds of values, the Life Value and all the other relative values. What happens if one person feels that his relative value supersedes the Life Value of another? That relative value has now become immoral and can result in the third type of conflict. If the value is acted upon it is unethical, and the act may also be a crime, or against the law. These kinds of conflicts *do* have to be resolved. There are many examples, and they all involve one person or group usurping the rights and possessions of another person and/or group. Stealing is an example: a criminal's relative value (I steal to gain possessions) conflicts with an innocent victim's relative value (I earn my possessions). When that criminal's relative value (desire for free money or possessions) supersedes someone else's Life Value, it is unethical and has to be resolved.[24] Crimes really come down to a disrespect of the Life Value of others.

Clashes can even happen between competing relative values that should conform to the "live and let live" rule, but, become disrespect for the Life Value. "You don't like vanilla ice cream! What's wrong with you? That's lame; you're stupid; I'll kick your butt!" Won't the vanilla ice cream "disliker"

---

[24] This is a very basic, philosophical explanation of why stealing is unethical. As often happens, it is not so simple in real life—or in literature. A must read is the classic novel "Les Miserables" by Victor Hugo which explores the morality of stealing to the protect lives of starving children.

rightly feel that his/her life is not valued? It happens often in sports. One person likes this team, one person likes another and they fight—and sometimes kill—over which is the better team. I don't like your team, so I don't like you. Your team is subpar, so you are subhuman. Cockroach! Therefore you can be attacked, even killed. Misfire!

There is also a possibility that the Life Value could compete with strong relative values in the same person. What if you have a relative value of liking ice cream, but that value is overpowering? It is making you fat and sick. In other words, you have allowed your relative value—love of ice cream—to supersede your own Life Value—your health. Misfire! Does this kind of conflict need to be resolved? Yes, sooner or later, one way or the other.

If misfires can happen between two people of the same culture who speak the same language, how easy might it be for *cross* cultural conflict to occur? Very easy. One aspect of the Life Value is the imperative to judge behaviors to see if they are life threatening to ourselves and others. But it is hard to be objective. Sometimes when cultures or customs are strange and unfamiliar it can be very difficult to view the people who practice them as equal human beings The ability to look at a person and differentiate between the value of his or her life and the value of his or her relative behaviors can be extremely challenging, especially if their words or actions seem disgusting or are dangerous. One of the most difficult things for us humans to do is to stay objective when we see members of any particular, identifiable group acting in ways that are disrespectful or life-threatening to others. We are tempted to paint all members of that group with the same brush. "Kill them all, let God (Allah, Buddha, etc.) sort them out." It is tempting, but wrong. Still, we are inclined to do it, because many of our attitudes are still very "tribal." These conflicts fall into the fourth type—those between Life Values.

The study of tribalism is beyond the scope of this book, but a simple, unscientific explanation of why human beings are tribal and tend to treat "outsiders" disrespectfully (demonize or dehumanize them), is useful for our discussion. I have run the following idea by several trained anthropologists and they say it is reasonable and probably sound.

For many millions of years, human beings lived in small bands or tribes, because it was the most sustainable (life protecting) way to live. With little technology, humans tended to settle in geographic locations—a valley, perhaps—that provided easy access to enough food, water and shelter to support their in-group. Those "societies" contained a fairly small number of people by today's standards.

So "Tribe A" is living happily in "Valley A" and all is well in the world. Over in "Valley B," however, where "Tribe B" lives, things have changed. There is population growth, or an environmental calamity like a fire or flood. There is no longer enough food in Valley B, and Tribe B starts to roam. Soon they begin to encroach on Tribe A's territory, and there is conflict. Before long it is serious. If we are in Tribe A, we have to stop the "invasion" to protect the resources needed by our in-group, perhaps by driving off Tribe B or killing its members.

Yet, it turns out (as we will discuss in more depth later) that we human beings are not natural born killers of our fellow humans. In fact, *life* is our primary and universal value. So how do we deal with the conundrum? What do we do? We create an artifice. We allow ourselves to believe that those "others" from the encroaching tribe are...not human. We *de*-humanize them, and perhaps demonize them (project an inherent evilness upon them). Now it becomes slightly easier to attack and, if necessary, kill them. It's an imperfect trick, but it works to a certain extent, especially when emotions like fear, anger, disgust, etc., work to overwhelm our organic ability to reason. The artifice doesn't always work perfectly, however; people often feel guilty or depressed when they dehumanize others, especially if it results in violence and killing. But they do it, and have been doing it for thousands of years.

And we are still doing it. People don't have to be of distinctly different tribes to have conflict. Almost any real or imagined cultural or behavioral value deemed objectionable by members of one group can lead them to rationalize themselves into violating the Life Value of those "others." As we have discussed, people do it over such arbitrary differences as a favorite sports team—or because they grew up on a different block, as in the case of some youth gangs.

Two people can just decide to dislike each other for *no* apparent reason and decide to fight. There may be a person in your neighborhood whom you dislike. You probably speak the same language. You both may have the same basic economic and social standings. Your kids may go to the same school. You may share a basic ethnicity and culture. Yet, you can still find something objectionable about him or her that causes profound dislike. Would you kill him over it, however? You may think not. But the neighbor-on-neighbor killings in both Rwanda and Kosovo, just in the late 1990's, should make you pause with caution. You *think* you wouldn't do it, but you might—or, under the right circumstances, your neighbor might do it to you!

The point here is to drive home the Life Value vs. relative value dynamic. There is a real danger—for and to all of us—of we humans succumbing to the seductively easy mistake of using relative values (rather than the Life Value) as a criteria for judging the *inherent* worth of another human being. When a person's behavior is not "equal," or does not conform to what is considered "good," then it is as if the person himself is not equal or worthy of being alive. When people of one relative value system (behavior, culture, religion, etc.) see people of another relative value system as "unequal" human beings (read *sub-*human beings), the trouble begins. Then, it is a surprisingly short time before the killing can also start. It is happening too often to be ignored.

It should be no surprise that it is so difficult for us to keep the difference between the Life Value and all of the other relative values clear, particularly when we are in conflict or under stress—*or afraid*. Stress and fear are mental and physical challenges throughout life. However, clarity on the relationship between the Life Value and other relative values—especially under stress—is very important to our ultimate happiness and well-being. One reason it is difficult to maintain the differentiation is philosophical: The very concept of a absolute, universal and qualifying value is either misunderstood or rejected by many. Even academicians and scholars—perhaps *especially* academicians and scholars—have had a very difficult time making value judgments about cultural behaviors. Whether consciously or subconsciously, they have accepted the cultural relativity shibboleth which asserts that all cultural values are equal, just different, and should be respected. In an effort to be "unbiased" and "fair," this position is especially—and often zealously—applied to cultural values that are not their own. They have also bought into the concepts of moral relativism and the blank slate. This perspective is misguided, of course. There *is* a universal and objective value, that value is life, and some relative values can be very wrong. How do we know? We know because they obviously violate the

Life Value of self and/or others, and cause hate, conflict, fighting and killing.

Remember that this is an emotional and highly nuanced subject. Just being aware of the Life Value doesn't always make it easy to respect all life and objectively evaluate the relative value of all other cultures or behavior sets—celebrating them when they are life affirming and rejecting them when they are not. That is often a tough job. We sometimes won't succeed, although most of us do a pretty good job much of the time. That is at least partly because it is in our nature. One of the purposes of this book is to clarify the Life Value in hopes that it will help us get even better at maintaining a fairer balance of regard between self and others—particularly under stress. Conscious knowledge of the Life Value, even for those who are already naturally adhering to it, can be extremely helpful in keeping that moral compass calibrated. If your goal is to become better at using the Life Value as your "true north" and to maintain a reasonable balance of concern between self and others, it will require some practice. It is worth it, if you believe that peace and well-being for all of us is a worthy goal.

One tool would be a better vocabulary of values, morals and ethics. I have used the following simple "values, morals and ethics lexicon" with thousands of Marines, law enforcement officers, martial artists and even scholars. Many have found it valuable. Harvard professor and science writer Steven Pinker called it a "masterpiece of values education." I don't know about that, but I offer it here as a review of what we have been discussing:

Values. As presented previously, values are "things that have an intrinsic worth in usefulness or importance to the possessor," or "principles, standards, or qualities considered worthwhile or desirable." It is important to note that, although we may tend to think of a value as something good, virtually all values are morally relative—neutral, really—until they are qualified by asking questions such as, "How is it good?" or "Good to whom?" The "good" can sometimes be just a matter of opinion or taste, or driven by culture, religion, habit, circumstance, or environment, etc. Again, almost all values are relative. The exception, of course, is the Life Value. Life is an absolute value. We might take this point for granted, but we all have the Life Value, or we would not be alive. Life is also a dual value— self and others.

Morals. Moral values are relative values that protect life and are respectful of the Dual Life Value of self and others. The great moral values, such as truth, freedom, charity, etc., have one thing in common: when they are functioning correctly, they are life protecting or life enhancing for all. But they are still relative values. Our relative moral values must be constantly examined to make sure that they are performing their life-protecting mission. Even the Marine Corps' core values of "honor, courage and commitment" require examination in this context. Courage can become foolish martyrdom; commitment can become irrational fanaticism; honor can become self-righteousness, conceit and disrespect for others. Our enemies have their own standard of honor, they have courage, and they are surely committed. What sets us apart? Respect for the universal Life Value sets us apart from our enemies.

Ethics. Ethics are moral values in action. A person who knows the difference between right and wrong and chooses right is moral. A person whose morality is reflected in a willingness to do the right thing— even if it is hard or dangerous—is ethical. Ethics are important because they are moral, life-protecting actions that are respectful of others—all others. Ethics are consistent with mankind's universal values as articulated by the American Founding Fathers— "human equality" and the "unalienable right to life."

The word "moral" is derived from Latin; the word "ethic" from Greek and Latin. Consider the following definitions; they are very close.

Moral: pertaining to, or concerned with correct principles or rules, or, the distinction between right and wrong.

Ethical: pertaining to or dealing with morals or the principles of morality; pertaining to right and wrong in conduct.

Some people use these words interchangeably because their definitions are so similar. However, please note the words "principles" and "rules" in the definition of moral, and the word "conduct," in the definition of ethic. It may be true that the distinctions seem unimportant, but we can use them to differentiate between morals as *ideas* and ethics as *actions* based upon those ideas. This is not the only way these terms can be explained, of course, but it certainly is more useful than not having a distinction at all. I would enthusiastically welcome an even better explanation of values, morals and ethics if you have one. Remember, too, my audience. I often work with Marines, law enforcement officers, and other people who want to be ethical under extreme stress. They don't need fuzzy terms and lofty ideas; fancy semantics don't help them. They need something straightforward that they can *use*. And, I would argue, so do the rest of us.

Now that we have our vocabulary clarified, it must be said that the definitions above are not typical. In fact, the language of values is often very imprecise. For example, there is confusion between the terms "values" (those things that are worthwhile to us individually or collectively), and "traits" (similar human characteristics that we may share to one degree or another). Even the word moral is usually used in a relative context—some things are moral if done by one person, but, not another. Or some customs are moral in one culture, but not another. It is time that we stop the moral and cultural relativism and have an objective way to judge whether an act is ethical or unethical that applies to all of us—after all, we are all equal human beings as it pertains to the value of our lives. The point of objectivity, therefore, is the Life Value; and I argue that we require clarity in our every discussion of values, morals and ethics.

Yet, as we have said, the words morals and ethics (and sometimes virtues) are still often used interchangeably. I argue that this lack of clarity is more than incorrect—it can be dangerous. As we have proposed, the definition of ethics is a balanced respect for self and all others in our every action. Granted, it is virtually impossible to judge infallibly who may or may not be affected positively or negatively by any given action; but we have to have some kind of guide.

Consider the following metaphor: When we walk into an unfamiliar shopping mall and are looking for a particular store, don't we look for a directory and a map? The first thing we need to find on the map—perhaps even before we locate the store itself—is what? It is the little arrow that says "you are here." We cannot use a map to get where we are going without knowing where we are. So how do we "know where we are," or *who* we are as an inherently moral person and "do the right thing," even under great adversity? We must practice activating a conscious awareness of the Dual Life Value way *before* we act.

Once we are traveling on the rough terrain of life, the path to moral behavior may seem different or more difficult (or even easier) than we thought it would be based upon our study of the map. But the map is necessary—and a true north is indispensable.

So far, we have covered some rather nitpicky philosophical ground. If you recall, my audience typically has neither the time nor patience for a scholarly philosophy lesson. The good news is you don't really have to memorize it! If all of the above seems a little too philosophical, here is a vignette, called "The Bully" to explain the terms in a more down-to-earth way.

The Bully

You are a kid in the schoolyard. You see a bully. He sees himself as the "top dog." That perception is a relative value: He may believe it, but everybody else surely doesn't. But, that is fine. Who cares what he thinks? Until the day that his relative value supersedes the Life Value of another kid—in other words, when the bully picks on and/or punches the other kid. This is wrong and must be stopped. Here is the rule: *relative values, no matter how "great," cannot supersede the Life Value.*

You see the bully picking on the other kid. You feel—in your gut—that this is wrong. Congratulations, you are moral. By the way, most people are moral—they know the difference between right and wrong and prefer the right.

Now...you see the bully picking on the other kid. You overcome the "freeze," you overcome the embarrassment, and you go tell a teacher. Congratulations! You are ethical. Ethics are moral values in action.

Now...you see the bully picking on the other kid. You overcome the "freeze," you overcome the fear, and you go to the aid of the kid being bullied. You put yourself at risk. Congratulations! You have the makings of an Ethical Warrior.

Have you ever heard the term "Irish late-bloomer?" I am a pretty big guy now, but when I was in eighth grade, I was the smallest kid in the class except for one girl named Barbara. I was also a precocious little kid who liked music and theater. I was a prime target for bullies. Of course, one singled me out. He insisted on fighting me in the schoolyard in front of everyone—with boxing gloves on to make it "fair." I was petrified; I knew that I would be killed. But what could I do? I had to fight.

Enter John Eager. John was a recent transfer from a tough public high school where he had gotten into some trouble. He did not know anyone at his new school, and was kind of a loner. It turned out he was a drummer and somehow found out that I was a guitar player. Later, we ended up starting a band and becoming close friends. We both needed friends.

John was bigger than I, and when he found out about my "boxing match" he did one of the most amazing things that I have ever seen in my life. He offered to fight the bully first to tire him out. Now *that's* a friend! I said no, but John insisted (and I really did want him to, I admit). He fought the bully long and hard, was beaten badly and eventually lost. The bully went on to make short shrift of me. I think John got hurt more than I did, because he lasted so much longer. That incident in the schoolyard changed my life. I have been a bully-hater and an admirer of Ethical Warriors, like John Eager, ever since.[25]

Unfortunately, bullying does *not* get stopped on a daily basis in school yards across the world…too often because some morally confused and/or cowardly teachers and administrators do not recognize and/or acknowledge the Life Value violation. And it also doesn't end in the schoolyard. Almost all problems in our society are caused by bullies — those who would supersede the Life Value of others with their own relative values. We need Ethical Warriors to counter bullies. John Eager was my first encounter with a true Ethical Warrior.

There is more about Ethical Warriors in Part II. In the meantime, please note that we can help ourselves and others to become ethical through training and encouragement that reinforces our inclination to act consistently in accordance with our moral values.

---

[25] Unfortunately, John was killed in a drunken driving accident when he was 18. He was driving.

That begs the question, "Why wouldn't we act ethically in the first place?" The answers are simple: Fear, or embarrassment, or philosophical confusion; or we might simply "freeze" under the stress. That is why it is important to be aware of—and believe in—our inherent moral sense. It is not certain that there is one formula that works for everyone, but there appears to be one that works for most people.

The "ethical formula" is: Moral + Physical = Ethical.

That's right, we have to perform moral acts—and actually *practice* being ethical and acting in a self and others protective manner.

Most people are moral—just like those of us in the schoolyard who know that the bully is wrong. But we may not be consistently ethical—not when it gets difficult, scary, dangerous or wealth-threatening. Then we find it much harder to act in accordance with our moral principles.

And it isn't just that we, usually moral people, are constantly falling off the wagon and doing unethical things—although that does happen. We are often passively unethical—when we don't speak up or act against the immoral actions of the bullies of the world. We see them in the schoolyard; we do nothing because we are scared. We see them in business; we do nothing because we are frightened and confused and worried for our jobs. We watch them gain high positions in government and politics; we do nothing because we feel helpless (and may secretly hope that we will somehow benefit personally in some unequal way if we vote for them).

Remember, we are still quite tribal. Why do some bosses of failing companies unfairly take big salaries, perquisites and "golden parachutes" for themselves and their inner circle while the other employees suffer? Why do politicians vote themselves better benefits than their constituents? Why do some people accept unfair political advantages? Because they can. It is not necessarily wrong to look after yourself and your in-group; we often hear that charity begins at home. But advantages have to be obtained fairly and reasonably. They should not be gained at the *expense* of "outsiders." Refusing unfair advantages is hard; the tribal mentality is not easily overcome.

But most of us are trainable. We are already inclined to be protectors by our human nature. Life is the only basic and universal value. But it is not a selfish value; it is a value of closely balanced self and species preservation where species-preservation has the slight edge.

One thing that really helps people follow their moral inclinations (behave ethically) under stress is...being physical. Here's my direct experience: It's easier to make a physical person moral than a moral person ethical. More about that later. For now, let's tackle the subject of adhering to the Dual Life Value principle as we deal with people we don't like and people outside our "in-group." Again, it is not easy.

Chapter 4
All Others

"The best way to destroy an enemy is to make him a friend."
- *Abraham Lincoln*

"Ye have heard that it was said, 'Thou shalt love thy neighbour, and hate thine enemy,' but I say unto you, love your enemies, and pray for them that persecute you."
- *Matthew 5:43-44*

I was in an airport in Buenos Aires, Argentina when I was struck by the sight of a huge kiosk with people collecting relief effort donations for victims of a hurricane that had occurred the previous year...in Haiti. I am unhappy to say it, but it never occurred to me that the people of Argentina could be so concerned about people, not of their "in-group," who lived thousands of miles away, and that the concern would remain long after the tragedy had disappeared from the newspapers. Shame on me. The fact is that Argentineans—and many other people everywhere— *do* care about people that they don't know. Some are very passionate about it. The good news is that there is evidence to show that our compassion may actually be growing. Steven Pinker has written that "we are getting nicer every day."

"Over the millennia, people's moral circles have expanded to encompass larger and larger polities: the clan, the tribe, the nation, gender, other races, and even animals. The more one knows and thinks about other living things, the harder it is to privilege one's own interests over theirs. The empathy escalator may also be powered by cosmopolitanism, in which journalism, memoir and realistic fiction make the inner lives of other people, and the contingent nature of one's own station, more palpable—the feeling that 'there but for fortune go I.'"[26]

There is now a great deal of literature on how far we are capable of extending genuine feelings of concern to others. It may certainly depend on such factors as an individual's capacity for compassion, resources, direct vs. indirect knowledge of those others, etc. But it is clear that we can and do have empathy for others not of our immediate "in-group." I also like the fact that the circle of concern seems to be growing. Can you imagine a global relief effort a mere 100 years ago? How would it measure next to what we saw for the 2010 earthquake in Haiti, or for the 2004 and 2011 tsunamis that impacted Asia and Japan? Or the magnitude of present day efforts to protect whales and dolphins (not to mention the Busuanga Wart Frog)? I can't.

---

[26] S. Pinker (March 2007). A History of Violence. The New Republic Magazine. Read also The Better Angels of Our Nature: Why Violence Has Declined. Viking (October 2011)

It appears that as technology allows us to experience and become familiar with beings outside of our culture or in-groups, our Life Value balancing mechanism begins to figure those others into the mix—and that advances a kind of moral evolution. Technology facilitates our ability to humanize "those others" who were "out of sight, out of mind." We *see* and read and empathize—we are reminded that those other people "hurt like we do, want like we do and hope for their children, just like we all do."

While the science of evolution is outside the scope of this book, it is comforting to consider that the self-others balancing mechanism is organic and can adjust as we understand more about people far outside our traditional "in-group." It is not so hard, at least in the abstract, to think that people living on the other side of the world are pretty much just like us. Granted, they possess different languages, cultures and skin colors, perhaps, but they are fundamentally the same in that we would probably act like they act if we were in their environment; and they would do the same if the circumstances were reversed.

Consider the orphan adopted into a foreign family who, while retaining his or her biological heritage, adapts fairly easily to a new environment. Both biology and environment play into who we are (nature *and* nurture), yet our moral sense and human equality seems to be more essential than either—or at least the same—regardless of our genes or our place on the globe.

Differences are natural, too. Identical twins are genetically the same, but still different in many ways. Harvard Professor of Psychology Jerome Kagan once noted that "Although humans inherit a biological bias that permits them to feel anger, jealousy, selfishness and envy, and to be rude, aggressive or violent, they inherit an even stronger biological bias for kindness, compassion, cooperation, love and nurture—especially toward those in need."

Why is it sometimes still so easy to hate outsiders? As we discussed, the tribal mentality exists; it may have developed as a survival mechanism over the millennia that we were hunters and gatherers. And it persists. Tribalism and viewing outsiders as threats are still atavistic for most societies today. Both tendencies evolved to serve the Life Value; they were functional, though sometimes cruel. Our ancestors, who did not view newcomers (i.e. Valley B interlopers from the previous chapter) as threats, did not last long. Tribalism and aggression toward strange beings and potential competitors for resources kept us alive. Through natural selection, strong tribal "protect the home turf" drives became our *modus operandi*. Just because it is now a less than necessary proclivity due to advances in civilization doesn't mean that xenophobic tendencies may not still be imprinted in our human nature. It may take further evolution of our moral sense to eradicate it. We can also consciously overcome our natural, now deleterious, drives with education and practice. Our fear of outsiders only because they *are* outsiders is almost like a psychological appendix: it no longer has a necessary function, but it sure can cause trouble if it gets inflamed or bursts.

A conscious adherence to the Life Value provides us with a beneficial, more humane path. Clearly, Valley A can accommodate many more people with today's technology than it did in tribal days. Regardless, more people in our "in-group" provides diversity in the gene pool (which is species protecting). It also provides a greater breadth of knowledge and skills in the community, opportunities for division of labor, not to mention a wider availability of people to fall in love with and/or with whom to reproduce. But, until our morality evolves to the level that tribalism is a recessive inclination, we have to use reason to make sure our small group tendencies don't cause a misfire of values. Again, training helps, as we will see.

In the meantime, let us tackle the biggest obstacle: caring about our enemies. This seems to be totally illogical and self-destructive. The concept of protecting others, especially those not of our "in-group," can be difficult enough. Risking our lives for others, even strangers—as firefighters, police officers and military personnel do—can seem heroic, but difficult and even counter-intuitive to some of us. But, caring about, much less protecting, our enemies may seem totally irrational. However, it turns out that there is a great measure of satisfaction in a life lived according to the precept of protecting *all* others.

Similar to the way we sense the truth of our human equality, when we protect others we sense that we are "doing the right thing;" and that results in a feeling of nobility and serenity. The subtle thing about being a protector is that the reward is virtually intangible—spiritual, even. *And we receive that reward regardless of whose life we protect!*

Here is a surprising story from Iwo Jima; it is the third life-changing story that Robert Humphrey told me in that San Diego classroom. He called it:

The Story of the Japanese Prisoner

Most Marines know the story of Iwo Jima. One of the "dirty little secrets" of that battle was that the Japanese did not believe in taking prisoners, as surrendering—even when wounded—was considered a violation of the warrior code of Bushido.[27]

Unfortunately, some Marines began to follow suit with the killing of wounded, captured or surrendering Japanese soldiers. There were also atrocities, including cutting off ears and other body parts, as well as, the tromping out and collection of gold teeth.

One day on patrol, Humphrey and his men came upon a young, emaciated and

---

[27] This, in my opinion, is an over-simplification and perversion of the true Bushido concept of service to the emperor—and by extension, to one's nation. It is just another example of how a relative value can "misfire" and become rationalized and disconnected from the Life Value.

clearly frightened Japanese soldier in a torn, filthy uniform emerging from a cave waving a white flag. This, in and of itself was unusual, as Japanese soldiers rarely surrendered. One of the Marines, convinced that this was some kind of trick, raised his rifle to kill the young Japanese soldier. Humphrey found himself ordering the Marine to put down his weapon. A short, intense confrontation occurred between Humphrey and the Marine. But good order and discipline prevailed and the Marine lowered his weapon. It turned out that the Japanese soldier's surrender was genuine and he was taken safely to the rear. The prisoner also turned out to be of some intelligence value.

Humphrey thought little of the incident at the time. There was so much killing before the occurrence—and so much afterward. But the experience stayed with him. He explained: "On Iwo Jima it was life or death every minute of every day. There was unavoidable killing every day. When I saw that Japanese boy trying to surrender and understood that this was perhaps the only time that I didn't have to kill, I took the opportunity. *I believe that action saved my humanity.* Like most veterans of Iwo Jima who survived, I was deeply affected by the experience. Yet, I never suffered the profound depression and shell-shock (PTSD) that some of the others did. I attribute it to saving that boy's life. Protecting my enemy, if you will."

Humphrey had told me this story, but I had almost forgotten about it until an incident that occurred near the end of his life. Humphrey had been invited to speak before a world conference on values at Drew University. He was a big hit at the conference, as most of the speakers were presenting from purely academic or theoretical perspectives. Humphrey's real world experiences and stories stole the show. When he opened the floor up for questions, I thought of something that I had never asked him. I wanted to know, what he considered the proudest achievement of his very eventful life. Was it getting to the national tournament as a collegiate boxer? Was it earning a Purple Heart medal for being wounded on Iwo Jima? Was it his Harvard Law Degree? Teaching at MIT? His work overseas during the Cold War? Or in Vietnam? His work with schools? He thought for a moment, and then said, "Remember the story of the Japanese prisoner? I believe saving that Japanese soldier's life was my life's greatest achievement."

Besides the emotional impact, this story is very interesting because it describes how the "fog of war" can lift, and a sense of moral clarity take its place, even in the most horrendous of circumstances—war on Iwo Jima. Humphrey said he believed he could effectively handle combat for two reasons. The first was that he had had a good moral upbringing by his parents; that was further clarified by his experiences during the Depression, which made it clear what was "really important" in life. It wasn't wealth or material things—because there weren't any! It was helping each other.

The second reason was his time as a semi-professional boxer. We will discuss later why warriorship and sport fighting are not the same. Yet it is clear that the physical adversity, particularly the hits to the face, were extremely helpful in training Humphrey to manage the stress of real combat. As a result, he was better able to control his emotions, including fear and hate, and the Life Value mechanism was then able to operate. This is just another reason why martial arts are vital to Ethical Warrior development and part of the training regimen. As we will see, martial art training has been demonstrated to help Marines find and orient their moral compass, particularly under the stress of war.

Life, thankfully, is not a killing war for most of us, and for that we can be grateful. Yet, we do have to make self and/or others choices *all the time*—often under duress. How can we learn to be ethical without the "benefit" of getting shot at? A physical-moral approach may also work for us. It starts with the philosophy of the Ethical Warrior.

First, let us apply the Life Value feeling and logic in the case of our enemy. We know that he or she values their own life and the lives of their loved ones, the same as we do ours. The enemy's reason for fighting may or may not even be his or her own. During World War I, front line soldiers often felt that they had more in common with the enemy soldiers in the trenches opposite them than with their own rear echelon troops and the people at home.[28] Enemies facing each other are both at a life and death awareness. Their cultural, political or emotional differences may spontaneously reveal themselves as relatively unimportant and the shared adversity can create an actual bond between them. This phenomenon occurred between British and German soldiers in the trenches of France during World War I who laid down their weapons to celebrate Christmas together.

The Christmas Truce

"English, come over!" we heard one of them shout. "You no shoot, we no shoot."

There in the trenches, we looked at each other in bewilderment. Then one of us shouted jokingly, "You come over here."

To our astonishment, we saw two figures rise from the trench, climb over their barbed wire, and advance unprotected across No Man's Land. One of them called, "Send officer to talk."

---

[28] A. P. Linder, 'Magical slang: ritual, language and trench slang of the Western Front', http://www.firstworldwar.com/features/slang.htm

I saw one of our men lift his rifle to the ready, and no doubt others did the same—but our captain called out, "Hold your fire." Then he climbed out and went to meet the Germans halfway. We heard them talking, and a few minutes later, the captain came back with a German cigar in his mouth!

"We've agreed there will be no shooting before midnight tomorrow," he announced. "But sentries are to remain on duty, and the rest of you, stay alert."

Across the way, we could make out groups of two or three men starting out of trenches and coming toward us. Then some of us were climbing out too, and in minutes more, there we were in No Man's Land, over a hundred soldiers and officers of each side, shaking hands with men we'd been trying to kill just hours earlier!

Before long a bonfire was built, and around it we mingled—British khaki and German grey.[29]

What processes, psychological, biological or chemical, happen or have to happen in the brain for us to maintain focus on the Life Value, keep our relative values in perspective, and hold our emotions in check under extreme stress? A detailed, scientific explanation is unimportant for our purposes. We

---

[29] The Christmas Truce, By Aaron Shepard, Printed in Australia's School Magazine, Apr. 2001 and http://www.aaronshep.com.

know that some of us can do it, at least part of the time, even during war. Why can't we all do it more reliably and more of the time? What holds us back? Both logic and those same emotions hold us back. Logic first: What if we respect the other person and he or she takes advantage of our good nature? What if he or she merely uses our respect for them against us? No, we have to make sure that he or she is also willing to live and let live, or we are at risk by not being suspicious. We may even use our suspicions to justify a pre-emptive attack—in other words, get them before they get us.

The second reason is our emotions. Emotions are very powerful stimuli to things that we believe are either beneficial or harmful. When working effectively, they give us extra energy to either enjoy or avoid these opportunities or situations. For example, happiness is an autonomic, maybe even instinctual, preparation of our minds and bodies to accept and take advantage of good things. Fear prepares our bodies for bad things; we freeze if that protects us, fight if that protects us, or flee if that protects us. Other emotions, like shame, may protect others—we feel shame because it is a strong deterrent to anti-social behavior, that is, actions that will harm others. But, though emotions *can* be useful, they are not always so. Screen doors are useful, but not when it is freezing outside (and not on submarines). The value of an emotion can be judged by how it supports the Dual Life Value in context.

I used the word "instinctual" above, but humans are not totally instinct-driven; we do have free will. Therefore, it is probably more accurate to say that human morality and ethical behavior are "instinct-like," and controllable by reason. I have also heard that morality is "intuitive." But, intuitive implies that ethical inclinations to respect life come from "out of nowhere." I suggest that morals and ethics come pretty reliably from our human nature. But human morality is "instinct-like" in that it can be over-ridden by strong relative values (i.e. my tribe is human; all others are sub-human). Human morality can also be eclipsed by strong emotions—fear, desire for revenge, disgust, culture-shock, anger, etc. That is why it is necessary for most of us to train ourselves to be more consistently ethical—especially under stress. We need to *practice* self-control and self-discipline.

Soon after I joined the Marines, I was visiting my college buddies over a weekend and looking forward to a party they were throwing at the fraternity house. As soon as I arrived, I sensed something was wrong. There was no talking and laughing as I would have expected. Music was playing but the rest of the house was eerily quiet. I soon found out why. There was a drunken bully in the kitchen making everyone uncomfortable. I quickly stepped in like a good Marine and took charge of the situation. "Look pal, it is obvious that you are unwelcome here, why don't you leave?" I started escorting him to the door. When we got to the front porch he resisted. I pushed a little harder and he turned around and took a swing at me. I blocked the blow and counter punched him to the jaw, knocking him right off the porch onto the front lawn. Then I did a very bad thing. I jumped down after him and hit him again when he was clearly down. More than thirty years later I am proud of that first punch—and still burn with shame for the second one.

Later, friends said that I was justified in hitting him again, making sure he wouldn't get up and continue fighting, or pull out a weapon...yada, yada, yada. But if I was so right, how come I felt—and still feel—so bad?

Today, I believe that my moral compass is more finely calibrated and the Dual Life Value is clearer in my psyche. I don't think I would let my emotions override the Life Value as they did so long ago on that porch. At least I hope I wouldn't. But I realize how strong emotions—like bloodlust—can be under stress, so I continue my practice so that I never have to live with another shameful feeling like that experience.

Is it a scientific fact that a calibrated moral compass will consistently trump counterproductive emotions? I don't know for sure but I do now have decades of experience observing the interplay of values and emotions under stress in life and death situations, and in many different cultures. We want to be constantly looking for additional research to help us verify that a combination of moral clarity and training can help us avoid inappropriate emotional responses. It may not be possible, desirable or even healthy to totally suppress our emotions, whether they are autonomic or instinct-like or some combination of both, but reason must also plays its vital role.

It is said that there are six primary emotions: Love, Sadness, Joy, Anger, Fear and Surprise. Each emotion has both positive and negative aspects. For example, love can be a positive compassion or a negative obsession; sadness can be genuine sympathy or negative depression; joy can be the contentment from doing the right thing or the hedonistic ecstasy of an addict; anger can be the revulsion to an immoral act or an inappropriate response to something you just don't like. And so on. We have to have emotions. The key is control and balance. Emotions can threaten one's well-being, or the life of self and others, so it is beneficial to develop the ability to harness or override them when necessary. Emotions, or at least actions that may be catalyzed by the emotions, are controllable by reason. It takes maturity, experience and work.

What kind of work is required? To protect yourself from the fear of a physical attack you could live in a safe place, buy a weapon, learn martial arts, support the Police Benevolent Association, etc. There are many possibilities. None of them are 100% sure to work, but with a little effort you could have a reasonable amount of freedom from the fear of physical harm. Preparing yourself wisely for financial dangers is also prudent and possible. Again, it may not be easy, but a rational response to the possibility of financial problems would be to lower your expenses and/or raise your income rather than live in constant anxiety. When it comes to the emotions, we can't always control embarrassment, excessive pride, shame, or feelings of inadequacy or even anger. But with constant focus on the Life Value we can practice keeping the balance. Without it, the job is a lot tougher. If all values are relative, than how do we prioritize? If one focuses on the Life Value emotions are easier to control. Humphrey used to say, the only important value is life; everything else is just a detail. My mother often says, "If it isn't a matter of life and death, I am not going to worry about it." Great pieces of advice which are not always easy to follow.

But that is the point. With all of the options and distractions, with the impossibility of making sure every action or decision strikes the exact right balance between what is good for us and good for all others, living according to the Life Value is sometimes very hard. I suggest, though, that living without a clarified awareness of the Dual Life Value is even *more* difficult. Ignorance is not bliss in this case. Without a foundational, objective value—and having a balanced regard for self and all others as a premise for our existence—living a consistent, happy balance can be just about impossible. Even with a strong sense of the Life Value, and a consistent effort to allow it to guide us, strong relative values can still cause conflict. However, with some effort and some common sense, we can create an approach that allows us to live with, or resolve, conflict between competing values, as necessary. This is the realm of conflict communication and conflict resolution. From a values perspective, choices break down in several distinct ways that bear repeating. Is the conflict:

1. **Between competing relative values?** All conflicts may not have to be resolved. Not every conflict between relative values *can* be reconciled—nor needs to be. I may never like vanilla; you may never like chocolate. But let's put those differences in perspective. The fact that we have different relative values has nothing to do with the Life Value—unless we make it so. Emotionally, we tend to disrespect people who have values we don't like. But we can use our powers of reason to keep our emotions from overriding respect for the Life Value. In fact, showing respect for others often stops conflict—without even addressing the differences between our other values.

2. **Between relative values and the Life Value?** When disrespect for another's relative value turns into downright demonization or dehumanization of that person, it is clearly unreasonable. We can't confuse the value of a life with a relative value or behavior— particularly if that value or behavior, in and of itself, is not life-threatening. Most values aren't; even the really irritating ones usually aren't life-threatening. If we are tempted to dehumanize someone because of a relative

value, we must recalibrate our moral compass and resist. Avoid the other person, if necessary, until reason can re-establish itself over the emotions. If the other person is disrespecting or threatening us, and we feel that the conflict must be resolved, then we show respect for that person's life, even though it is difficult. That may be the point of reconciliation. Arguing over relative values usually doesn't create a point of reconciliation. How could it? Differing relative values are the *source* of conflict. Police officers, for example, have to address conflicts like this all of the time. When we train them in conflict communication, they practice seeing the suspect from two distinct perspectives. Address the immoral and illegal *actions* appropriately, but still show basic respect for the *Life Value* of the perpetrator. The Life Value is the only reliable common ground in most conflicts.

3. **A Life Value conflict?** Life Value disputes are often the result of de-humanization, and can involve a misfire of a moral value. As discussed, some cultural, religious or behavioral values are very life protecting for some but not for all others. This causes one person or group to disregard the Life Value of (de-humanize) those not of their in-group and rationalizes the taking of resources or privileges at the other group's expense. This often turns into a violent downward spiral.

The other group, in turn, rightly feels threatened. They say: "How dare you treat me and mine as less than you and yours? *We* are not sub-human, *you* are sub-human." We dehumanize our enemy right back so that it doesn't feel as wrong to hate or attack or kill them—for the moment at least.

What seems clear is that respect is the key to conflict resolution. But respect for what? Respect, respect, respect. Nowadays, all people talk about is respect. The number one reason gangbangers kill people (including each other) is "he didn't show respect." But they have it all wrong and don't know why. It is not respect for relative values, like everybody thinks it is, but respect for the Life Value of self and *all* others—regardless of the conflicting relative values. However, people often do the opposite, partly because they were indoctrinated with a seemingly benign and "respectful" philosophy called "cultural relativism," which we alluded to previously. Cultural relativism proposes that "all cultures are equal, just different, and you have to respect them all." Sounds nice, but in practice it can be deadly. What happens in reality is that relative values start to become overriding…and *if you don't respect mine, I'll…*(fill in the blank) *attack you, arrest you, fine you, shun you, politically correct you, and, if I judge it necessary, kill you.*

All relative values are *not* equal, they are moral when they protect self and others, but immoral when they don't respect all others. It is not logical to respect or even tolerate the relative values of all others without qualification. That would lead, inevitably, to *more* and increasingly violent conflict, almost always including (perhaps, requiring?) demonization and/or dehumanization. The dehumanization process takes place on different levels and to different degrees. But the bottom line is that if a relative value supersedes the Life Value of even *some* others, it must be re-examined. We must strive to train ourselves, if necessary, to separate the Life Value (always worth respecting) from the relative value of behaviors (*may or may not* be worth respecting). Again, showing respect for the Life Value helps reconcile conflict between relative values, or make it moot. We re-calibrate — and live and let live.

One day I was driving in Bayonne just about ready to get on the New Jersey Turnpike. Suddenly, I came upon an altercation right before the toll booth. There was a van stopped in the middle of the road and a man was yelling at the driver. The yeller had at least five dogs of various sizes on leashes in his hand. It was hard to figure out exactly what had caused the ruckus, but it seemed to be something about the man and his dogs trying to cross the street (not at a marked pedestrian crossing, by the way) and the driver of the van almost hitting one of the dogs. The van driver was trying to apologize calmly and get on his way, but dog man was having none of it. It was soon apparent that the dog man was a bit mentally unbalanced—and violent. Every time the van driver tried to pull away the dog man would jump in front of the van and pound on the hood. He ripped off a wiper blade; then he started to pull off the license plate.

I tried to intervene, but no one was listening and the dogs started jumping on me. Not necessarily wanting to get into a physical altercation in my suit (or get dirty dog paws on my pants, starched shirt and tie), I hurried back to my car for my cell phone to call 911. I had just gotten the police dispatcher on the line when dog man walked over to the side of the van and cold-cocked (punched without warning) the driver in the face through the open window. "Oh no," I thought, "Here we go." I told the dispatcher to hurry up and get a cruiser over here and ran back to the van just as the dazed driver exited the vehicle...with a baseball bat in both hands and started swinging wildly at dog man. I waded into the frenzy and took the bat away from the driver, ran back to my car, threw the bat into the back seat, and went back to try and get between the two who were now threatening to kill each other. It was obvious that van man, though angry and hurt by the punch to his head, was more rational than the other guy. I looked at the dog man and said to myself, "Just drop him." But I couldn't. It just didn't feel right to hit him. Anyway, by that time, some other people had come by to help me, including a decorated Army Sergeant in uniform (where did *he* come from?). The police arrived shortly thereafter. I gave my statement and my opinion on who was more at fault, got in my car and left. And then it hit me, "Holy sh*t, you just saved the bad guy." Weird, how this protector stuff works sometimes. I feel pretty good about that one, though.

Clearly, the ability to put truly offensive or threatening behavior into perspective and still respect—and protect!—the person in the wrong is not easy. But, I hope it now seems reasonable and desirable.

Some people's relative values are difficult to understand, or may even seem downright offensive from another's point of view. There are behaviors that are definitely nutty, and may be caused by a mental imbalance—which was probably the case with dog man from the story above. Some behaviors are criminally immoral, of course, and the perpetrators have to be stopped, captured and, possibly, killed.

But all difficult to understand behaviors are not necessarily immoral—or illegal. Sometimes they can make good sense if we understand the context and reason for them. One of the ways to gain the ability to remain objective is to be curious. Unfamiliar cultural and behavioral values often have a moral, life-protecting reason behind them. The life-protecting reason may not always be readily apparent and/or that reason may no longer be viable under current circumstances. But with a little investigation, a little "cultural detective work," as Humphrey used to call it, sometimes we can get to a point of respectful understanding.

Chapter 5
Respect

"The worst form of inequality is to try to make
unequal things equal."
- *Aristotle*

"All the people like us are We,
And everyone else is They."
- *Rudyard Kipling, We and They, 1926*

The moral "gray areas" intrinsic to conflict between and among different cultures, religions, tribes, behavior sets, etc., are of concern to all of us. Any book on ethics must address the cross-cultural aspects of conflict, at least to a certain extent. Without attempting to trivialize the countless unique and often wonderful aspects of the many world cultures, we can try to de-mystify them in a way that allows us to attain a fairly objective perspective.

One way to look at culture is to view it as a set of relative behaviors used by a particular group of people in a particular environment to live effectively. Simply, we can say:

Life Value + Environment = Culture

As we discussed, Life Value plus equatorial heat may equal a culture that wears grass skirts. Or, Life

Value plus arctic cold may equal a culture that wears fur coats. Or, Life Value plus frequent sandstorms equals a culture that wears turbans and veils.

In other words, the Life Value is the constant; the relative environment is the variable; and people do their best to live in that environment by developing cultural values and customs that help them survive. Cultural values can reflect any demographic variable: weather, geography, topography, food supply, availability of water, etc. Cultural values may also be shaped by human variables such as empathy, wisdom, ignorance, largess or greed, the appearance of good or bad leaders, and many other factors. Cultural values are mostly effective and, at least, fairly successful. As the population of the world has grown exponentially so also have relative values. One reason for that explosion, of course, is our increasing ability to shape the environment through technology, cooperation and division of labor into one that sustains life for more and more people. That is not to say that every life is happy and that every life is respected. As with moral values, even life-sustaining technology can lead to misfires. It can lead to alienation and disrespect from—or for—the organic balancer of the Life Value: the individual. Certainly, technology can have unconsidered negative side effects on the environment and the lives and health of some. We have to be mindful of the Life Value as we use it. Technology for technology's sake (building it because we *can*), if divorced from the Life Value, can have very unintended—and harmful—consequences.

Isn't it logical for the design, creation and use of technology to proceed from our Life Value? It may be said that technology is a culture in and of itself, in that it adapts to the environment in ways that serve to protect and sustain our lives.

The ubiquitous cell phone is a perfect example of a life-protecting technology—especially for those of us with children. This fantastic device has enabled concerned parents to stay connected to their wandering teens. The handy phones are instrumental in saving/protecting the lives of countless lost youths. However, the phones can be a terrible distraction for some kids. Speak to any teacher in a school that does not allow them. The number of teens who appear to be hopelessly addicted (I do not use the term lightly) to the devices grows, and the number of incidents of teens literally refusing to turn their cell phones over to teachers/administrators when caught, is alarming. Many teens openly assert that they would rather be written up or suspended than lose their phone for any period of time...misfire.

Most technologies and virtually every cultural and behavioral value have, at their source, a life-protecting or life-enhancing role. Technology is certainly intended to make life easier and more pleasant, and so are most cultural values. Customs such as the prohibition against eating certain foods, the veiling of women, extreme differences in male and female domestic roles, seemingly exaggerated and arcane notions of hospitality, arranged marriages, etc., were probably initiated for what was deemed as very sensible reasons at the time and in the environment in which they developed. "Don't eat these foods!" Why? Perhaps at a time before the proper preparation of these foods was scientifically understood, people often became sick from eating them. So, a cultural value developed that forbade the eating of that particular food. That might beg the question: "Well, we know how to prepare these foods properly today, so why wouldn't we eat them now?" Perhaps out of *respect* for that value's long-time role as a life-protecting (moral) relative value. Isn't this reasonable?

Here's another cultural behavior to think about: A little imagination can take us to a time when men roamed for days in the wilderness. When they came upon an encampment of strangers they often encountered two things: grandiose hospitality...and veiled women.

Hospitality to strangers represents the very truest of our others-protecting inclination. It is also what might be called reciprocal altruism—if you extend hospitality to others, you may expect it to be extended to you when you need it. Thus, a cultural behavior or custom is born. But why the veils? Again, perhaps, respect. Respect for the women who may not want to be ogled by a bunch of guys who just spent two months out in the desert. And respect for the men themselves, who may be biologically distracted by women who are part of another family—a form of "out of sight, out of mind." If this sounds strange and unnecessary today, you might then wonder why there is still a custom in many cultures, even today, for brides on their wedding day to be...veiled. Respect.

As for the men, there is at least one reason why it is obvious that in the Arab world the traditional *keffiyeh* headdress is often worn. Just like their American cowpuncher counterparts wear bandanas, men wear them to shield themselves from direct exposure to the sun, as well as to protect their mouth, neck and eyes from blown dust and sand.

Some relative cultural values may seem illogical, hard to understand, wrong, dangerous and downright scary to outsiders. Contributing to the confusion and the possibility of conflict is the fact that some cultural values may have historical or environmental reasons that are not immediately apparent or may no longer seem logically valid. Have you ever wondered at the indiscriminate firing of weapons at weddings? This practice was common for many years in...Ireland. But it probably was inspired by the French tradition of *charivari*, a noisy folk custom involving the banging of pots and pans outside the homes of newlyweds meant to tease and encourage the bride and groom to consummate their marriage. When guns became more available, the banging just got louder. The firing of weapons after marriages has been banned in most parts of the world and will probably be banned everywhere eventually—it is just too dangerous, unless you are out alone someplace in the middle of, say, a desert. But the compulsion persists (as well as the noise) in many places in the world in the form of...tying tin cans to the back of the newlywed's car as they drive off to seek conjugal bliss.

These are just a few examples and corresponding conjectures, albeit based upon the Life Value view. There are many customs that made good sense at one time, but may be overdue for revision. Yet they can still be understood and respected in context to a reasonable extent, until they are naturally adapted to new realities or dropped all together. Why would we retain any cultural value or custom after it becomes moot, unnecessary or even dangerous due to new information or technology? One answer might be that certain values were at one time so life-protecting for everyone that they actually seemed like universal values. They are maintained out of respect and remembrance of the good those particular values once provided. Are they still necessary? Perhaps not, but they may still be very psychologically difficult to discard. I would argue that others, such as burning witches and honor killings, should be banned immediately and universally. But, it is important to use the Life Value as a foundational premise when analyzing the relative value of any cultural behavior—and certainly not uncontrolled emotions.

Analyzing unfamiliar or seemingly strange customs for their life-protecting roots is a matter of practical sense, as well. It helps people of different cultures reconcile their relative values and focus on the Life Value that they share. After all, as strange as some cultures are to us, our culture may seem strange to others. While some of us may not want to veil our daughters in *burkhas*, others may not want their daughters wearing very short skirts—or cavorting for the cameras in bikinis (or less) during Spring Break. We would all have understandable points.

Here we ought to clarify the difference between the words "empathy" and "sympathy." Empathy means that we *understand* how others feel. Sympathy means we *agree* with how others feel. We can have empathy for people whose customs we don't necessarily agree with. If a cultural value seems strange or wrong, we can try to discover the "life-protecting" reasons that spawned the development of that value before making a judgment. Sometimes, an unfamiliar value will feel very sensible—maybe even better than our own—once we understand the history behind it. Be a cultural detective.

My wife is from Japan and I'm from the United States. When we got married, I had to quickly learn some new cultural values in order to stay out of the doghouse. For example, I now live in a home where shoes are not worn indoors. If you did not grow up with this custom it is often irritating, especially after you have laced up your shoes only to realize that you left your wallet in the upstairs bedroom. Although it took me quite a while to get used to it, I have come to believe that it is a much cleaner, healthier habit that allows you to relax and exercise your feet. You can imagine my surprise one day when the doorbell rang and I heard my wife let in a plumber to look at something in the basement. Clomp, clomp, clomp he went, straight through the kitchen, and down the stairs. Ah ha! I confronted my wife and asked her why she had let him wear his boots on our polished hardware floors. She looked at me as if I was crazy and said, "He works with heavy tools, he has to wear his boots to protect his feet." Drat! Foiled again by the superseding Life Value.

One often hears disparaging things said about under-developed countries regarding their ability to "modernize" their cultures and societies like we in the developed countries have done. One hears statements such as, "They are ignorant and backward and nothing can be done about it." Or, "What do you expect from a bunch of ignorant _____s? (Fill in the blank). They are like animals." This is disrespectful and de-humanizing. And dangerous. When conflict occurs these sentiments can lead pretty quickly to immoral statement like, "We should just bomb them back into the stone ages." Or: "We should just nuke 'em until they glow. Turn the whole country into a big piece of glass." You hear this kind of thing from "so-called" educated people, too. It is appalling, ignorant and amazingly arrogant. As we know, cultures are relative. From one perspective or another, different cultures may seem to be at relatively different stages of development. But, the differences are not in the people themselves; they were driven by the different relative environments. In the West, we tend to look down on the people of underdeveloped countries as being slow and backward—somehow defective. How soon we forget...

Imagine it is 1775. A spaceship lands in Philadelphia. "Superior" beings (let's call them the "Visitors") with "modern" values and fabulous technology (especially weaponry) emerge from the ship. They approach Benjamin Franklin and say: "Earthling, we have been watching from outer space. We see that you are being treated unjustly by these British beings. It is wrong and we want to help you become free."

"Sounds great; we're all about liberty," says Ben.

"OK, then," say the Visitors, "let's get started. But, before we do, we need to ask about this slavery thing you have in the South. What's that all about? We couldn't possibly help you and condone that. You need to stop that right now."

Ben says: "Funny you should say that. Old Tom Jefferson was talking about that just recently. He is saying that 'All men are created equal,' and that this is the proper perspective for our new government to take. He does have slaves himself, though, so he and many others are going to have to sort of transition out of the slavery thing. We figure it will take about 100 years and probably a Civil War to do it, and maybe 620,000 or so deaths. But we are committed to abolishing slavery."

Shocked, the Visitors say: "100 years! We need to get back home. We are not going to hang around on this crummy planet for 100 years. You need to do something immediately.

"And by the way, while you are at it, we don't see any provision for your female beings to vote. What's with that? While you are abolishing slavery, you might as well give women the right to vote while you are at it!"

"We hear you," says Ben. "But, that kind of thing takes time, too. We figure, let the Civil War go by, let everything calm down for a while, say, another 30 or 40 years. Then we'll introduce and ratify an amendment or something. How does that sound?"

"That sounds ridiculous! You are talking 140 years!" say the Visitors. "Why don't you just get some kind of Civil Rights Act together, clean up all these antiquated ideas at once and kill all of these birds with one stone?"

Ben is apologetic: "You really don't understand how people are around here. We have lived a certain way for hundreds, maybe thousands of years. Many of us realize that a change is due, maybe past due, but it takes time for people to change—even when the changes can be good. You have to be patient. Slavery? 100 years. Woman's suffrage? Another 40. Sweeping Civil Rights legislation? Maybe another 40. When you step back, 200 years for all of these changes seems pretty fast. Don't you think?"

The Visitors say: "Well...we were thinking more like 3 or 4 years. Hey, we gotta go." They get back into their space ship and take off.

Sound familiar? In a way, this is the way we can sound to people in developing countries who are supposed to be our allies. We need to get over the culture shock, be a little more patient and understanding and, especially, a little more respectful.

Robert Humphrey, in his nearly fifty years of cross-cultural conflict resolution, created this group of admonitions that any reasonable person might find helpful when exposed to a different culture. He used the acronym **RECTIFY** to help us remember the steps that can often be used to understand and reconcile cross cultural differences:

> Reason – Find the reason for the difference.
> Exaggeration – Stop the exaggerations.
> Compare – Compare the alleged difference(s) to your own culture for forgotten similarities.
> Toughen-up – Don't let the alleged difference(s) make you negative. You will suffer the most.
> In – Join "in" with the local people until you can acquire some understanding of the difference(s).
> Facts – Get the facts! Don't believe everything you hear.
> You – You may be the problem! Be aware of your own small intolerances, especially if others from your group are enjoying the cross-cultural adventure. If it turns out that you are the problem, go back to the "T:" Toughen-up!

In the real world, of course, some cultural or behavioral values can be totally irreconcilable. Despite the tempting promises of Cultural Relativism leading to utopia, the truth is otherwise. When people view the relative values of others as objectionable, they are sometimes quick to judge those values as wrong (whether or not they are truly immoral), and view the people who practice them as unequal and unworthy of respect. But remember, it is not often that cultural differences are truly intolerable. They can be different, uncomfortable, maybe a bit shocking, or even seemingly stupid or dangerous—yes, but usually tolerable. It is a lack of respect for our human equality (our Life Value) that people find truly intolerable. If, after investigation, the cultural values of an individual or group still seem invalid (or no longer valid under the present circumstances), you can still seek to activate a mutual acknowledgement of the Life Value between you.

The Life Value approach works fairly reliably to resolve unnecessary conflict. Even with...teenagers. I have teenagers and, I have to tell you, they have a culture that I often find uncomfortable, sloppy, disrespectful, stupid and dangerous (of course, like most parents, my selective memory tells me I was never like that; this generation is *way* different from mine). But, after I put my emotions in perspective, I have to admit that, though I may dislike their behavior, I do still love them. I do not consider them human only when they act the way I like them to act and subhuman when they don't. They are the same person all along. This ability to separate the relative value of a particular set of behaviors from the objective value of life is key. We also have to train ourselves to apply this distinction outside our "in-group." It is not easy, but it is reasonable. I would suggest, in this shrinking world, that it is imperative. Acknowledging this distinction between relative values and the objective value of life will lead to reduced conflict and increased happiness for you and others. Remember, "cultural appreciation" may not always be enough to quell cross-cultural conflict. (That is the myth of cultural relativism.) However, mutual respect for the universal Life Value often can and does!

While it is helpful to know something about different cultures with which we are likely to come into contact, it isn't always possible or practical. When training military and law enforcement personnel for performing their duties in the real world of conflict, we often have to acknowledge that it is impossible to be experts on every culture we may encounter, especially on the fly. Can a Marine at a checkpoint who is suddenly confronted by an agitated individual be expected to know his language? His religion? His tribal affiliation? (Much less the respective cultural values associated with each?) Impossible. When Marines get the call to duty, they may not even know in what country they will be operating. Similar challenges could present themselves almost anywhere in the world to any of us who travel. They could even confront us here at home in our own, increasingly multi-cultural home nations. For example, can police officers be expected to know the nuances of every culture of every person they might encounter? Knowing something of the cultures of the people in the service area is important and useful, but in a, diverse environment like a city, how could he or she know about them all?

The question becomes: Is it necessary to know everything about every culture before you can help resolve conflict? Can respect for the Life Value be enough to help address the explosive short-run kind of conflicts that we might run into on a daily basis? Consider this incident from the Iraq War. I have gone to great lengths to verify the accuracy of the story; and I believe it to be true. I have spoken to the officers in charge of this area when this incident occurred, and while we have yet to locate an official AAR (After Action Report), they all agree that it happened.

The Corporal and the Iraqi Funeral Procession

During the early stages of the Iraq War, violence was a daily occurrence and tensions were high between the local populace and the coalition forces. In a rough area outside the main city of Ramadi, a squad of about a dozen Marines, led by a corporal, was on patrol. They became aware of a major disturbance brewing out of sight behind a building about a block away. Suddenly, a large, menacing crowd came around the corner right toward them. Immediately, the Marines went on high alert. The Iraqis were yelling and wailing and a confrontation seemed inevitable. Yet, somehow the corporal sensed that what he was seeing was not an attack on his patrol, but an Iraqi funeral.

Instead of opening fire on the agitated crowd, he ordered his men to ground their weapons, take off their helmets, and bow while the procession passed. An amazing thing happened. Immediately the atmosphere changed, the tension dissipated, and the group passed peaceably. Not only was there no fighting, but that gesture of respect led to good relations between the Marines and the people of that area from then on.

The question I asked myself when I heard this story was, "How did the young corporal know to do that?"[30] He didn't speak the language; he couldn't have known much about the Iraqi culture. No one could have blamed him if he had interpreted the

---

[30] There is a similar story in the January 17, 2005 issue of the New Yorker magazine entitled "Battle Lessons" by Dan Baum. In that article, the protagonist is an Army Lieutenant Colonel. Regardless of who performed the heroic and respectful act, or how many times similar incidents may have occurred, the moral of the story is the same. You don't necessarily have to be a cultural expert to act successfully to avoid cross-cultural violence.

situation as a threat and eliminated that threat. What he did was counter-intuitive and certainly seemed downright dangerous—and brave. So, how did he make what turned out to be such a wise choice?

While you consider that, think also about a police officer on the job here in one of our own cities being confronted by an agitated group of people. The people appear to be of foreign descent; they are speaking with an accent. But which accent? Are they Middle-Eastern? Hispanic? From which country are they? Every country has slightly different cultural values and customs. Can this overwhelmed police officer be expected to know them all? Impossible. So what is the best approach?

One of the great oversimplifications in dealing with cross-cultural problems is the thought that conflict is just a translation problem. For example, when Marines are in a foreign country, it might seem helpful, perhaps vital, to have enough interpreters and cultural experts. The theory is that if we can just communicate with the local people, things will go more smoothly. But is that really the core issue? Think about this: the people in that land speak the same language and are familiar with each others' customs and cultures. So what are they fighting about? Here in our own country, we share a basic culture and language—at least most of us do. Does that mean that we all get along and that there is no friction, conflict or fighting? Of course it doesn't! So what is the root problem, and are interpreters and "cultural sensitivity experts" really the key to solving it, or are they only tools that *may* help?

Wouldn't it be wonderful if all it took for people to get along was for them to speak the same language and to be sensitive to each others' culture? Nice dream. In fact, there is literature that suggests that 12.5% of the time we do not understand what someone is actually saying even when we are speaking the same language, same dialect, and have the same education and profession.[31]

When I first started martial arts training in Japan, I was a big, tall Marine, 25 years old or so—hard as a rock; and dumb as a stone. The only problem was that the smaller, and in many cases much older, Japanese teachers could throw me around like a rag doll. They were nice enough to let me participate in the teacher's training sessions, but probably only because I was an exotic (and large) punching bag on whom they could try out their techniques. Perhaps they thought that if their stuff would work on this big lug, then it would work on almost anybody.

One day, one of the really tough guys came to the little *ryokan*[32] where I was staying and called me out for some one-on-one training. He did not speak a word of English, and I spoke only rudimentary Japanese, but I knew what this was all about. He was offering to teach me the basics of the martial arts so

---

[31] John Nance. Why Hospitals Should Fly. Second River Healthcare Press; 1 edition (January 15, 2008)
[32] A ryokan is a traditional Japanese Inn.

that I could better understand what was going on in the instructor classes. We went to a small shrine, and he beat me half to death (my left elbow hurt for about eight years). After training that night with Hatsumi Sensei, he took me out to a Chinese restaurant for dinner, and showed me how to drink as hard as we trained. Then before we went to bed, we walked and ran up and down the paths between the rice paddies, learning all kinds of weird ways to move—sideways, backwards, stealthily, quickly. Finally, exhausted and still a little intoxicated, I fell into bed—after I washed my muddy and bleeding feet.

That became my routine. Up in the morning, read for a while, eat lunch, train with my new taskmaster in the afternoon, meet or train with my teacher in the evening, eat and drink at the Chinese restaurant (the place was run by a family in which there were four daughters—one really cute, as you may recall from the story in Chapter 1), run in the rice paddies, and then go to bed.

That man taught me the fundamentals of Japanese martial arts. We got along brilliantly, despite our virtual inability to communicate (except by body language). I called him *sempai*, which means something like mentor or big brother.

Several years later, after I was married, I invited him to visit me in America. I was very excited because I would finally be able to have my Japanese wife translate all of the little nuances of communication that we had never been able to share before. I was going to cement a life-long bond with this fellow martial artist with whom I had shared so many long, body-wracking sessions.

I picked him up at the airport and drove him to my house in New Jersey. We went into a long conversation with my wife translating—kind of—and I thought that it was all very grand. That night in bed, however, my very circumspect wife asked me gently, "Is this guy really your friend?" I said, "What? Of course, he is my friend. He is my *sempai*; we are great buddies." Then she told me that the great relationship that I had with this man who I had respected for so many years was really not what I thought it was. Without going into detail, because I still value the things that he taught me, I was left shaken by what she told me about what he had been saying. He really didn't like me that much at all—or at least he didn't talk as if he did. It turned out that the only things we had in common were the things we couldn't talk about. When it came to the physical martial arts training we were on the exact same page (or I was on his exact page). But we were philosophically incompatible. In fact, once he had gotten a few drinks in him he felt very comfortable degrading me and my non-Japanese culture. How he thought that this somehow was going to be favorably received by my wife is just one insight into the man's view of things.

The short moral of this story is that, in this case at least, when we were finally able to communicate and share details of culture it actually hurt our relationship. We were actually much better off when we couldn't discuss our relative values in detail. It turns out that he really didn't respect my cultural values—or me. That was the beginning of the end of our close relationship. It wasn't a language problem; it was a respect problem.

Of course, sharing certain cultural values may create a surface feeling of comfort and compatibility. If I know you are a Marine like me, or if we went to the same university, or follow the same football team, or have the same ethnic background, I may feel that our shared relative values should somehow bind "us" against "them." But the reality is that it is just not true that I will automatically have anything really important or vital in common with you without a mutual respect for the Life Value—even if you are an Irish Catholic, Villanova University graduate, who served in the Marine Corps and likes the New York Jets. Those things can definitely set us up to be mutually sympathetic—but only if I truly respect and value you and vice versa.

And this is important: The opposite is just as true, when you think about it. It is just as illogical to have an automatic prejudice against those with whom we do *not* share relative cultural values. It is sensible, and very possible, to respect each other *despite* our relative differences, because we share a more important value. But what is that more important value worth respecting? It is the objective value of our lives—the Life Value. That is the starting point. From an acknowledgement of a mutual Life Value, we have at least a fair chance of building a sympathetic, or at least empathetic, relationship—despite our obvious differences.

Let's face it; respecting relative values that we do not share is not easy. In many ways these difficulties are understandable. Some relative values just wouldn't work for us due to who we are and the environments in which we live. Some relative values work in some societies, but not in others. We explored this in a simple way with the fur coat vs. grass skirt analogy. Because cultural values are relative, often environmentally-driven, they certainly may conflict. The conflicting values can be deep-rooted and complex. This is both obvious and natural. Even people who are ostensibly of the same culture can easily disagree on their values. Are all Americans the same? All Japanese? All Arabs? Do we all think alike? Do we all have the same experiences? The same environments? The same relative likes and dislikes? No, of course not. We can find profound cultural differences between us and the people next door if we look. (I even have a neighbor who is a Yankees fan!) The truth is that even our own relative cultural or behavioral values can change or be inconsistent. I may go from a Mets fan to a Yankees fan (although, I doubt it) or I may change favorite foods, political parties, or even religions. I have a friend who is a "vegetarian" but eats fish—the last time I checked, fish weren't vegetables. So, shifting or contradictory relative values are fairly common.

But we still hold a strong, even fierce, emotional attachment to some of our relative values. This stubbornness can literally become deadly. People allow themselves to become obsessed with notions of "country," "culture," or "style." "Culture" is too often considered to be the definitive criterion of human worth. When this occurs, it almost always follows that those not of that culture somehow have less human worth. It is a frighteningly short road from there to disrespect, then conflict, and sometimes on to fighting or "ethnic cleansing." When "culture" is treated with more importance than life, the killing begins, sooner or later, guaranteed. In a more general sense, this means that anyone who puts something above life, whether it be culture, religion, or even money, honor, fame, prestige, etc., risks becoming dangerously disrespectful of others. In addition to the obvious error in philosophical logic, disrespect can easily create serious problems, especially when it manifests itself as a feeling that people of the other, "lesser" cultures are somehow lesser human beings. Those treated with disrespect inevitably become resentful— then, deeply resentful. This progression is only natural. You have heard the words "sticks and stones can break your bones, but words can never hurt you." It is not always true. Disrespectful words *can* hurt when they are a threat to one's livelihood (thus life).

Humphrey would tell of men who would fight savagely over words during the Depression, despite the commonly voiced admonishment not to do so. Humphrey explained the Life Value at work: "In those days of scarcity, jobs sometimes meant life or death. Calling a man a loafer or a thief could affect his (or his family's) chances of getting a job. Words like, 'Those Humphreys are all thieves and liars,' could be a life-threatening statement."

Resolving any conflict, but especially conflict complicated by cross cultural misunderstandings, is a serious challenge. Promoting peace? Respect for culture won't necessarily do it. Respect for others' religious beliefs won't necessarily do it. Our religions, cultures or behaviors may not even *be* reconcilable; the attempt to reconcile conflicting relative cultural and behavioral values might be hopeless. But, total reconciliation may also be mostly unnecessary. Even when cultures seem irreconcilable, conflict can often be resolved if a deeper, more fundamental value can be activated mutually — the Dual Life Value.

Before I summarize the mechanics of the Life Value theory in the next chapter, I would like to revisit the vitally important Hunting Story in Chapter 2. The insight of that sergeant regarding the true meaning of human equality has been invaluable to me, as it was for Bob Humphrey, in activating a respect for the Life Value in all of the many countries I have visited. In essence, that sergeant was saying that the value of the village people's lives *alone*, despite their hopeless destitution, made them equal to the relatively rich Americans in the truck.

The lead-up to the story is instructive as well. As you may recall, Humphrey had been charged with stopping Anti-American demonstrations at the U.S.

missile base in that poor allied country during the Cold War. Before Humphrey ever got into that truck with the old sergeant, both the American military authorities and the entire diplomatic staff had failed to successfully address the problems between the Americans and their allies in that foreign country. The story is interesting on many levels. There is the cross cultural element, there is the philosophical element, there is the values element, etc. There is also the scary element. The scary thing is that conflicts of relative values between people—even allies—can turn violent, fast.

When Humphrey first landed in that country, there was already rioting and low level sabotage. The first thing he did when he arrived was to ask the Americans what they thought of the local people. The response was virtually unanimous and shockingly negative. The local people, according to the Americans he interviewed, were "stupid, dumb, dirty, dishonest, lazy, unsanitary, immoral, cruel, disloyal, crazy and downright subhuman."

To get a balanced and fair view of the situation, Humphrey also intended to get the local people's side of the story. He planned to discretely survey the people in the area surrounding the American military base and ask them just two questions. The first question was "What do you want from us Americans?" And, two, "What can we Americans do to make for better relations?" Humphrey was required to coordinate with the American ambassador, so he discussed his plan with the staff at the embassy. When Humphrey presented the two questions the ambassador said: "Humphrey, this is a waste of time. I can easily answer those two questions. 'What do they want?' They want more money. 'What do they want us to do?' They want us to go home. There is no need for a survey."

Humphrey, trying to maintain an open mind, insisted on doing the survey. He had more than two thousand people questioned by local interviewers to be as certain as possible of getting candid answers. The results of the survey were astonishing back then. Not only did the people give different answers than those anticipated by the ambassador, they gave basically the same answer to both questions. Can you guess the answer?

Many people guess it correctly now, but in the 1950s the answer was a surprise. The local people didn't want more money, or even for the Americans to go home. They just wanted respect. They wanted us to stop looking down on them, to stop making fun of their customs and culture, and to stop looking disrespectfully at their women. They wanted the Americans to start treating them as equal human beings.

Humphrey thought, "This is wonderful!" He went back to the ambassador and said: "Sir, I have great news. We don't have to go home. We don't even have to give them more money. All we have to do is treat them like equals. We can do that. It's the American way! You know, 'all men are created equal.' I think it will solve the problems we are having here!"

Humphrey was met with condescending smiles of discomfort. One staff person said, "You know Humphrey, people are just different—some are tall and some are short, some are nice and some are not nice, etc." Another said, "This equality thing was used during the Revolutionary War as a tool to bond the common people against the British, but the man who said it was Thomas Jefferson, and he owned slaves." The ambassador ended the meeting by saying, "Humphrey, your results are beside the point. Our mission here is freedom, not equality. And you can't have both." Huh? (Sound familiar? We said almost the same thing at the beginning of the Iraq war, formally called "Operation Iraqi *Freedom*.") These highly educated, experienced, fairly open-minded diplomatic experts either did not understand, or did not believe in, the concept of human equality. However, they had no problem trumpeting the importance of their high relative value: *freedom*. By now, you probably see the mistake they were making and why previous attempts at conflict resolution had not worked.

To be fair, although Humphrey had studied the results of those surveys, he also wasn't sure of the import of what the people had said. The Dual Life Value concept had not been clarified at that time, and its significance was still unknown. It took an old sergeant, who looked like he had never had a philosophical thought in his life, to explain it. Bob Humphrey was able to resolve the conflict and quell the violence by telling the Hunting Story. It allowed him a way to make the truth that "all men are created equal" *feel* self-evident. The rules of law and the tools of diplomacy had not worked. Only the Life Value had worked. Had it worked perfectly? It seemed so; Humphrey got a standing ovation when he told the Hunting Story to a theater full of cynical and disillusioned Americans. But, Humphrey was a social scientist and very thorough. He did a follow-up survey a few weeks later. This time he surveyed the locals again, but also the Americans. For such a powerful story with such an enthusiastic reaction, the American results were surprising. They revealed that the American's attitudes had not changed that much—just a slight shift over the knife's edge from downright disgust to grudging tolerance. Disappointing.

But, the other surprise came when the local people's new surveys came in. They were off the charts positive. Just a little change from the Americans was enough. The people hadn't required or expected anything more than basic respect. The demonstrations ceased, the Americans stayed, and the missile base became operational. An even bigger surprise was that the story did not necessarily persuade the Americans, directly, to admit that the peasants' lives were equal to theirs. Rather, because it was delivered by a high-ranking government official, it seemed to reveal to the relatively lower-ranked GIs that they, themselves, were being properly recognized as equal to the upper-class Americans. Once they saw that they were finally getting that unequivocal equal respect for their lives, they were then ready to give it to the peasants.

An interesting historical note: the presence of that base was critical several years later as a leverage point during the Cuban Missile Crisis. It is scary to think of what might have happened if the base had been abandoned.

Chapter 6
The Theory

"In science it often happens that scientists say, 'You know that's a really good argument; my position is mistaken,' and then they actually change their minds and you never hear that old view from them again. I cannot recall the last time something like that happened in politics or religion."
- *Carl Sagan*

"Without commonly shared and widely entrenched moral values and obligations, neither the law, nor democratic government, nor even the market economy will function properly."
- *Václav Havel*

Robert Humphrey was refreshingly open-minded. He also avoided theorizing. Although trained as a lawyer at Harvard, he was really a social scientist. I think he would have identified with the Carl Sagan quote, above, and added "...or philosophy." Humphrey was a humble and honest man; he always qualified his ideas with statements such as, "from my experience," or "until we find a better way," or "this worked better than what we were doing," or "until more research is done," etc. Perhaps that is why he left the writing of the pure theory of the Life Value to others—thus this effort. I have taken on the responsibility of writing out the Life Value in philosophical terms with some trepidation, and with the caveat that what I have written is what I *believe* Humphrey was saying.

Humphrey also warned me about trying to write out the Dual Life Value in a book. He would say that, like the law, "it won't write." The simplest description of the Life Value is still too subtle and complex; it is not the work for a mere book. Business ethicist, Dr. Steven Olson, called the Dual Life Value theory "simplicity on the far side of complexity." We typically teach it multi-dimensionally in our Ethical Warrior and Ethical Protector courses.[33] So, although you may find some of the reasoning intriguing and the stories interesting, this book is really meant to be a companion to the actual training and *practice*.

Like most authors, I also reserve the right to change my mind or adjust my perspective as I learn more, and scientists discover more, about human nature and how our minds work. For now, the Life Value perspective first introduced to me by Humphrey has held true throughout my continuing years of observation, study and experience. Why is an awareness of the Life Value of such vital importance? It is important because the Life Value is the most powerful force available to reliably and peacefully guide and influence everything we do. Awareness of the Life Value, and the use of it as the qualifier of our

---

[33] Information on the Ethical Warrior and Ethical Protector training can be found at www.rgi.co.

other relative or subjective values, allows us to resolve conflict and promote happiness and well-being for ourselves and others.

So what's the hold up? Why don't we just do it? Good question—and we have already explored some of the reasons. G. E. Moore wrote, "It appears to me that in Ethics, as in all other philosophical studies, the difficulties and disagreements, of which its history is so full, are mainly due to a very simple cause: the attempt to answer questions, without first discovering precisely what question it is which you desire to answer."[34] Humphrey's first question was, "Why was there so much killing on Iwo Jima?" From there, he pondered the source of human conflict and sought clues within our human nature on how to resolve conflict, stop the killing and promote human happiness. He identified and clarified the Dual Life Value as the key. But people still focus on relative values, trying over and over again to reconcile conflicting relative values without stopping to ponder the question of whether that is even possible or necessary. Here's our question: can the Life Value be the objective point of reconciliation for all of the other competing, relative values?

If we are not in the military or law enforcement, the question may not be a matter of life or death. Yet we still deal with conflict on a daily basis, so a "common ground value" could be still vitally useful in promoting peace and harmony among us. So, why

---

[34] Moore, G.E. Principia Ethica, 1903 p. vii

do we stray from our natural connection to the Life Value, and how can we catch ourselves when we do?

It is now time for us to back up, review what we have discussed, and lay out the pure theory of the Life Value.

Human beings have many values: things that we think are worthwhile. Most of them are relative or subjective; that is, particular only to an individual or some others, but never to all others. As we go through life, our human nature-guided value system regulates itself "organically" as it is impacted by conscious and unconscious, internally-driven and externally-driven, proclivities and stimuli—in other words, our environments. An enormous number of elements go into driving our feelings and actions, but the qualifier of all of them is one particular value: the value of life. As we have discussed at length so far and will further elaborate upon, it is a *dual* value. For most of us, that duality consists of self and *at least* some others. Life is an objective value, because it is the one value we all share. Therefore, logically speaking, it appears that when we refer to others, it would have to mean *all* others. Otherwise, life would be a relative value. No one wants their life to be treated as if it were of relative value to another's.

Our ability to value the lives of all others is limited in practicality, but not in principle. In general, the Life Value is an organic mechanism that seeks a reasonable balance of regard between self and others.

The self-others balance functions best and seems to provide the most happiness and serenity when it is tipped slightly away from us and toward others. Yet, it is an organic system in that it operates from the inside-out, and cannot be safely imposed upon us by outside forces without risking the violation of our own natural rights. Outside forces (laws, customs, rules, etc.), however, can be used to address those of us who get too far out of balance—maybe like gutters address the bowling ball that can't stay in the lane.

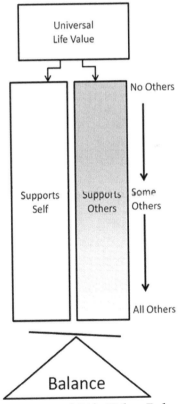

Figure 5 – Universal Life Value Balance

The Life Value concept is a dynamic system. It bids us to seek a reasonable balance of concern between self and all others, although the balance point can change according to the circumstances. Life is better for all when the balance is slightly tilted toward others, but you can't force it. It is up to all of us, individually, to seek the right balance at all times.

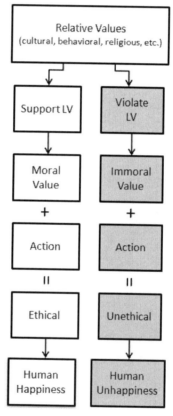

Figure 6 – Relative Values
LV = The Dual Life Value

For the most part, this natural balancing act works well. Although we have to contend with our emotions (including fear and a strong distaste for some relative values of others), the system is *controllable by reason*. We can often work our way back to a reasonable balance, just by activating an awareness of the Life Value within us. Some of the ways we can effectively find the balance is by:

1. Reading values stories.
2. Exposing ourselves to other cultures.
3. Volunteering to help others in need.
4. Sharing adversity with others.
5. Seeking out a mentor.
6. Gaining physical self confidence.
7. Practicing martial arts.

The goal and result of this dynamic self-others system is human happiness and well-being. When our relative values support and honor the Life Value of self and others, they can be called moral. If they violate or dishonor the Life Value of self and others, they can be called immoral. Actions that proceed from moral values can be called ethical. Actions that proceed from immoral values can be called unethical. Ethical behavior results in human happiness. Unethical behavior often results in human unhappiness.

It is not always easy to know in advance what thought or action is life-protecting and life-honoring, but we appear to have an innate moral sense in that regard. We can almost always *feel* the difference between right and wrong—unless we are one of the few percent of people who lack empathy for either the self or others' side of the Dual Life Value. Personal experience and guidance from others can also help us be ethical.

It is a dynamic process, however. As we learn new things, meet new people and experience new environments, we see that our opinions and feelings can evolve and that the results of our actions have broader and broader implications. The Dual Life Value remains the qualifier of our values. No matter how we feel, life is still the absolute value. We must consistently, from the inside—but also, if necessary, using guidance from outside sources—calibrate and re-calibrate the moral sense that guides our actions.

Attaining a reasonable balance between the well-being of ourselves and the well-being of others is a challenging and ongoing endeavor—known also as the art of being a good person, or a person of character or virtue (a virtue is a great moral value). All things being equal, a balance between self and others is the most reasonable way to live. Certainly, some people are too selfish, and some people are too selfless. They are the exceptions. They represent the tail ends of the bell curve that represents all of us almost all of the time. Most of us are pretty close to the middle, and that has made us an amazingly successful species, even with all of the mistakes, including the wars, genocides and other calamities (including political and economic ones) that some of us—the exceptions—have brought upon the rest of us.

Think of a bell curve: in the "fat" part of the curve you have most of us—we keep a reasonable balance of respect for self and others most of the time (Figure 7).

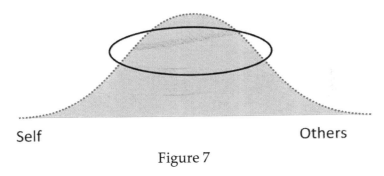

Self   Others

Figure 7

In times of "plenty" we tend to shift a little more to the self side, perhaps indulging our personal desires (Figure 8).

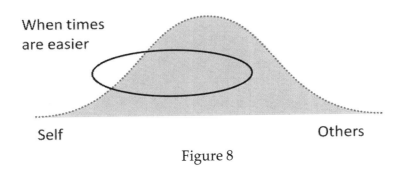

When times are easier

Self   Others

Figure 8

When times are hard for all, we tend to shift more to the "others" side, pull together, and help each other (Figure 9).

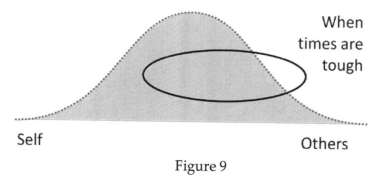

Self   Others

Figure 9

These are just illustrations, of course. In actuality, we are all shifting back and forth, billions of us, many times every day. If you drop a piece of litter on the ground it is a little easier for you. But, if you put the litter in a trash can; it is a little better for you and others—for many reasons when you think about it. It is a beautiful organic system—supported by our relative cultures, social rules, man-made laws, and even military rules of engagement (ROEs), tactical directives etc. Some people have an unbalanced Life Value. Some, either temporarily or chronically, don't value their own life. The range goes from having low self esteem to being suicidal. Other people are missing the "others" side of the equation. These persons range from merely selfish to conscienceless or even sociopathic, and some are criminals. Many healthcare professionals refer to this "super-selfish" condition as "antisocial personality disorder," which is characterized by a non-correctable disfigurement of the personality that is now thought to be present in approximately 4% of the population.[35]

Are 4% of us really sociopaths? That seems very high to me. More reasonable to me would be the proposition that far fewer of us are actual, full-time sociopaths, but 4% of us can act sociopathically selfish based upon the situation or environment. An actual, full-time, sociopath is scary; regardless of how many are truly out there; just one can wreak terrible havoc. Most of us have a capacity to be moral most of the time; only a very few of us don't. The same goes for selflessness.

But the important thing is that it is organic—in that it comes primarily from the inside. This capacity can change within the individual. We may observe that some people seem to be "more hard-wired" than others; that is, more naturally or consistently selfish or selfless. But even that is not 100% reliable. Some people who are ordinarily very "nice" and empathetic sometimes act with amazing selfishness—particularly under stress. Others, of whom we might not expect it, can be amazingly kind and selfless—or heroic. Consider this quote from World War II Marine veteran Humphrey:

"Human nature as I saw it on Iwo Jima is not such that everyone acts heroically. But human nature is such that the best of us humans do act heroically

---

[35] Stout, Martha, The Sociopath Next Door. 2005. pp6.

to save the group. Actually, it is even more sophisticated than that. When 'the best' is killed while trying to protect a group, the next best fighters tend to recognize that they are now 'the most capable.' Sometimes this assumption of leadership continues right on down the line to those who are the weakest, and they too will step forward toward that horror of possible death when other lives in their 'in-groups' are threatened. That 'in-group' feeling is the trigger, but I found that this 'in-group' feeling is not hard to expand even across the historic barriers of ethnic hatreds spawned from bloodletting." [36]

Interesting!

Of course there are people who seem to be always at the tail ends of the bell curve—people who seem to be wired to be selfish (psychopathic serial killers, for example) or wired to be selfless (the Mother Theresas of the world)—but these are more like the exceptions that prove the rule. They have the Life Value, but the way it manifests itself is an anomaly—like a person who has blood, but it doesn't clot. They are different; most of us are more balanced. If you agree, doesn't it make sense to encourage a more active and rewarding expression of that balance by being conscious of the Dual Life Value?

---

[36] From private correspondence, 1996.

Certainly, people can be a little self-indulgent, but isn't that natural? Why shouldn't we enjoy things that will make us happy if they don't harm or deprive others unreasonably? That word "unreasonably" is relative, so we have to be careful. But our health, our entertainment, our personal ease and our security are reasonable pursuits. If we go overboard, most of us get a natural law reminder—we feel a little guilty. In another piece of personal correspondence, Bob Humphrey's son, Galen, wrote this:

> "Self indulgence has to be monitored to guard against misfiring into selfishness and/or showing disrespect for others. Personal health, security, entertainment, leisure time, etc., are human needs that fluctuate with the individual and are certainly relative for everyone. They all apply to the self side of the Life Value, but are not necessarily selfish behaviors.
>
> "However, my neighbor, seeing me take my Saturday back yard hammock naps may view my behavior as selfish and lazy. Why? Because my neighbor works twice as many hours as I in order to pay the bills of a large family. But, I may think, is that *my* problem? Unknown to my neighbor, I do not have the same bills because I sacrifice and do not have cable TV, an expensive phone, a newer model car, and my thermostat is monitored very carefully.

"Yet, my neighbor—totally occupied with providing for his/her in-group—only sees a napping sloth next door when heading off to a second job on Saturday. So, perhaps I can try to keep things friendly with my neighbor by helping a little with his/her situation if possible. It's work, but makes for a nice, guilt-free nap on Saturday afternoons."

The bottom line? Do not flaunt advantages in front of your neighbors who may not be doing as well as you. Finding the right balance between pride and humility is almost an art—and another key to "a better life." Particularly when times are tough, we need to recalibrate and find a new balance point. We need to pull together with others. Being self-indulgent during those times is being too selfish. The pendulum needs to swing to the group.

A broad awareness of the Life Value sometimes requires activation, as we are still somewhat inclined to be tribal. The "others" may initially be of our in-group only. Using the example of the two valleys in conflict from chapter 3, Valley B may be close to starving too, but to hell with them (even if they're my friends), I'm hungry and so is my kid. In order to decrease the suffering of the folks in Valley B we have to make a conscious, values-guided decision to help them, too, if we can. We will be both happier ourselves and more useful to others if we let the Dual

Life Value guide how we handle these kinds of situations, or...

Have you ever heard the phrase: "Let them eat cake."? It was supposedly spoken by "a great princess" upon learning that her peasants had no bread. The quote reflects the princess's obliviousness to the circumstances of her subjects.[37] Whether she actually uttered those famous words or not, there is no escaping that the selfishness of leaders in the face of their suffering people often sharpens the edge of the swinging pendulum. Did you hear that, Nicolae Ceauşescu, Saddam Hussein, and Moammar Gadhafi? Perhaps not; they all met a similar fate. There are other tyrants now in our world who may soon share their destiny.

The important thing to realize is that we have to analyze the relative situations of ourselves and our neighbors and *choose* to strike a fair balance. The balance cannot be over-imposed by outside forces; the balance is the natural result of billions of individual decisions and actions. We all have to contribute to that balance, each of us, every day, many times a day. Being consciously aware of the nature of the Life Value can be very helpful in making those daily decisions.

What is the best way to keep an appropriate balance under stress? We have found that it is a three step process:

---

[37] This phrase is often attributed to Marie Antoinette, but that is unconfirmed and unlikely. Nonetheless, Marie+
was eventually guillotined by the Tribunal of the French Revolution for treason.

1. **Clarify**. Spell out the nature of values, morals and ethics, as we are doing in this book.
2. **Activate**. Spark moral "feelings." One way is to use values stories so that the lessons are delivered with emotional impact into our "guts," not just our brains. Not surprisingly, a second way that activates the Life Value even more effectively is shared adversity. We often witness people pulling together under emergencies such as hurricanes or floods, and in Marine training we create shared adversity purposely so that the people in the group get "activated" to protect and support each other. A third way is mentorship. In my case, 16 years of Humphrey's example inspired my desire to be an Ethical Warrior.
3. **Practice**. To live a more consistently moral life requires a practice regimen (action program) for most of us. Continually reading values stories helps. Actively working with others under adversity, even if it is just working together at a soup kitchen, etc., helps even more.

One of Bob Humphrey's homework assignments was to practice being calm and forgiving in the car. Tough one! Especially when you run into a really bad driver. Another was to give out little nods of "hello" whenever you pass a stranger. This one can be tricky in tough areas or with members of the opposite sex.

With a little practice, however, you can learn to give just the right amount of acknowledgement and respect, and elicit a nice smile in return. It never fails to amaze me how a simple smile or nod of respect in response to my "hello" makes me feel so good; and this from a total stranger whom I will likely never encounter again. Why? We are *wired* to feel good when we respect others. Bob Humphrey always encouraged us to "give away your greeting, don't wait for a response, you have an unlimited supply, give 'em away." Why not? Try it; you will see that it makes for a "better life."

Patience and respect are also safer. These small gestures foster tactical awareness, as well as, a capability to preempt possible aggressive actions by others. You are paying attention, and they know it.

A third assignment was to attend a religious service of an unfamiliar denomination. That's a real eye-opener. Try it sometime.

But what is the most reliable method for preparing to be ethical under stress? My experience is that it is certain kinds of martial arts training. The life protecting actions are built into the training. Remember, ethics are ultimately moral-physical. Moral people may want to step up and do the right thing, but they often lack the physical courage and skills. Martial arts give them the necessary skills and perhaps most importantly, self confidence. It works *even if they never have to use them*!

Relative values come in three categories. The first category is values that conflict but don't compete. I like vanilla; you like chocolate. There is no reason for these two values to cause problems and they usually don't. The second category is values that have the possibility of competing. If we can only get one flavor of ice cream, we must compromise or negotiate and resolve the conflict. The third category is when a relative value competes with the Life Value: we are having vanilla because I say so, and if you don't like it, "tough!" and I will punch you. This kind of conflict must also be resolved and violence stopped.

Certain relative values are particularly respectful of self and others. We call them the great moral values or *virtues*. Whether they are respectful of self, others, or both, they are great because, when properly applied, they are life enhancing for all.

The Life Value is an absolute and universal value. We all have it or we wouldn't be alive. At birth, a baby's first action is to try to breathe and live. Even most people in comas will continue to live until the physiological infrastructure gives out. Where does this foundational Life Value come from? Nature? Nurture? Implanted by God? All of the above? I know what I believe. But, it doesn't matter—it just *is*. "A is A." That's how we know; it is part of our human nature. It is self-evident to the extent that if we don't have it, it is perfectly obvious to almost everybody.

The dual nature of the Life Value manifests itself in different ways at different times, but most of us are capable of finding the right balance most of the time.

An analogy might be our core temperature of 98.6 degrees Fahrenheit. Sometimes our core temperature drops and we risk hypothermia; sometimes it rises and we get a fever. These cases are anomalies; usually we can maintain 98.6 degrees on our own. Our Dual Life Value normalizing mechanism is similar. Sometimes we are too selfish, we feel bad about it, and we start to swing back towards center. Sometimes we are too selfless, we feel used or resentful, and we start to swing back towards center. Those who are criminally selfish (running a moral fever) may need regulation from outside sources, and we have law enforcement, courts and prison systems to step in. Overly selfless people may need help, as well. That is why there are professional therapists, and spiritual and religious advisors. On a more informal basis, we counsel our overly selfless friends to rest and to do something for themselves until they get the balance back.

We are morally obligated to prevent suicides if we can. Suicide is strongly discouraged in *all* moral societies. Why? Because life is of inherent (if sometimes unarticulated) value to all of us. The right to life is inalienable, which means that it cannot be withheld—even *you* can't deprive yourself of it, any more than you can ethically or legally sell yourself into slavery. In 1759, William Blackstone wrote in his Commentaries on the Laws of England, that suicide was a common law criminal offence—also referred to as self-murder—and harshly punished:

(T)he law of England wisely and religiously considers that no man hath a power to destroy life but by commission from God – the author of it. And as suicide is guilty of a double offence: one spiritual, in invading the prerogative of the Almighty and rushing into his immediate presence uncalled for; the other temporal, against the King who hath an interest in the preservation of all his subjects. The law has therefore ranked this among the highest crimes, making it a peculiar species of felony, a felony committed on one's self...

Archaic verbiage aside, it is interesting to note the two reasons stated above that proscribe suicide are both to the benefit of God and King—*others*, not the individual.

Prior to 1961 it was illegal to commit suicide in the United States. If you tried and failed you could be fined and/or jailed. The Suicide Act of 1961 changed that; suicide is no longer illegal, but in most states it is against the law to assist in another person's suicide. What has changed? The value of life? Or the ascendance of relative values?

That question is for you to consider. But, the point is that maintaining the Dual Life Value balance, with or without help, is vital. Can you imagine how difficult it would be to maintain a happy balance between self and others if we did not acknowledge that there was a moral 98.6 degrees?

A further complication that bears repeating is that our high moral values, *feel* like absolute values. Even if we are inclined to respect the lives of others, it is easy to make an exception if a particular person or group of persons violate one of our cherished high moral values. But that is a slippery slope. When we say we'll respect everyone unless they are of *that* religion or *that* color or practice *those* behaviors we have made life a relative value.

As science helps us to understand the actual workings of our brain, and the effect that both sociology and biology may have on our inclinations and proclivities, it seems that the Dual Life Value model of human nature will accommodate these discoveries and an understanding of it will help us live more fulfilling and happier lives. It also gives us a reliable tool for resolving natural conflicts between and among us. When we start to see instances when the balance is clearly not being struck, we can create mechanisms for dealing with the outlier behaviors.

But, please, not too many. In our increasing complex society we have more and more rules, regulations and laws. Why? Because most of our values are relative, and without a clearly and universally acknowledged "true north" it becomes unclear what "doing the right thing" is. It becomes a matter of not breaking the rules, not breaking the laws, or even more troubling, not getting caught—as many laws make sense, but many others are incomprehensible.

Figure 10 – Ethics and Laws

Remember, laws are impositions—they are outside forces meant to keep us from becoming too selfish (and sometimes, too self-less—that is why suicide is still taboo). In simpler words, positive laws are "outside in"; ethics are "inside out." If you want fewer laws, rules and regulations imposed upon you from the outside, try being more ethical from the inside.

Let's go back to the bowling analogy: if life were a bowling alley, laws would be the gutters. Ethical behavior is the alley, and our "bowling ball of behavior" can travel anywhere on that lane and be acceptably within moral bounds: balanced between self and others. We may not always get a strike, and we may have a few splits along the way, but we are mostly capable of staying out of the gutter and hitting at least some pins. An unusual analogy, perhaps, but it is important that we stay between the gutters and, just as important, that no outside force makes the alley too narrow for an average person to stay in the lane.

Sometimes the lane seems pretty narrow, or we are not sure exactly where the gutters are located. There are instances when we encounter moral "gray areas," and there is no easy way to navigate through the ethical challenges of life during these times. The fact that I wrote this book may make it sound like I am very sure of my values, morals and ethics. That is not the case at all. I know killing is wrong, but not always—sometimes it protects life. I hope I would never kill someone over a difference in relative values, but I, like most of us, have great difficulty respecting the human equality of people who have or exhibit relative values and/or behaviors that are immoral or illegal, or that I don't understand or just don't like. I know that disrespect for others is immoral, but disrespect for some of people's actions may not be wrong. When people act immorally, respecting their lives can be quite a challenge. The Japanese have a saying: "love the criminal; hate the crime." That is no easy task. It takes practice.

I am often challenged—sometimes aggressively— by experienced law enforcement officers who assert that this "respect the criminal," perspective is, well, "bullshit," to use one recurring term. "We respect the victim, not the criminal," they assert. Fair enough. I understand their point, but I must be clear that I am not saying to respect or to even remotely condone the criminal's actions. The so-called "hug the thug" approach to criminal justice smacks of the very kind of moral relativism that we must avoid. "If one is preoccupied with the insane, the neurotic, the psychopath, the criminal, the delinquent, the feeble-minded, one's hopes for the human species become perforce more and more modest, One expects less and less from people . . . it becomes more and more clear that the study of the crippled, stunted, immature, and unhealthy specimens can yield only a cripple psychology and a cripple philosophy."[38] What I am saying is that behavioral values are in a totally different category than the Life Value. We can deal professionally, ethically, and legally with the criminals' actions and still respect the absolute value of his or her life.

An anonymous peace officer posted the following comment to one of our Ethical Warrior articles about protecting our enemies:

"It is not our job to judge criminals, anyway, only to investigate and arrest them. If we fail to treat those we encounter with respect we have failed in our oath to defend and protect the United States Constitution. These individuals are innocent until proven guilty, not innocent until arrested. Having said that,

---

[38] Abraham Maslow on Sigmund Freud.

this does not mean you should sacrifice safety in how you respond to a suspect. Their actions dictate our response. Our response should always be lawful and exercised with as much respect as possible. Failing to treat your enemies with respect is a slippery slope that I refuse to tread on. It leads to failing to treat citizens with respect; failing to treat victims with respect; failing to treat love ones with respect and failing to respect yourself."

I couldn't have said it better. As we will discuss later, we also believe that a Life Value-based approach to dealing with immoral and illegal behavior is psychologically healthier for the warrior or officer, as it tends to ameliorate the effects of PTSD (Post Traumatic Stress Disorder). In that regard, here is one more interesting thing that came up in the dehumanization and PTSD discussion: nearly every person who has taken the time to write or tell me that they felt no obligation to show respect to criminals admitted that they, themselves, have or have had...PTSD! More about PTSD later.

One of the goals of this book is to inspire people—including myself—to keep a calibrated moral compass on the journey through life; and there is some pretty rough terrain out there. Adherence to the Life Value, however, does make the journey easier and psychologically healthier—especially when we are under great stress.

When it is a matter of life and death, our relative values seem to get put into proper perspective. But even when the situation is not a matter of life or death, the Life Value is of great assistance in keeping our priorities straight.

The fact is that everyday differences between right and wrong, morality and immorality, are often *not* a matter of life and death. But they sure can feel like it (ask the teenager who is told to hand over his or her cell phone to the teacher!). That is why our relative values sometimes misfire on us.

I recall times when I was lathered up about certain problems or indignities in my life and having Bob Humphrey laugh at me. When I would ask him to explain what was so funny, he would say, "Jack, that's just a detail; it's not like it is a matter of life and death." I guess after having lived through Iwo Jima, pretty much everything else is "just a detail." I have tried to adopt that attitude, because it is true. Our everyday life decisions are usually not as critical as choices made in war. Sometimes, it is just a matter of getting a reasonable balance of concern between self and others in order to live a good life. Getting that good balance between self and others—and maintaining it *by practicing*—is the art of living. For most of us, that means daily sustainment at home, at play…and on the job.

Chapter 7
Ethics

"Treating people with respect will gain one wide
acceptance and improve the business."
- *Tao Zhu Gong 500 B.C., Assistant to the Emperor of Yue,
2nd Business Principle*

"It has become dramatically clear that the foundation
of corporate integrity is personal integrity."
Sam DiPiazza, CEO of PricewaterhouseCoopers

Communication, Respect, Integrity, Excellence. Do
these sound like great core values? Of course! Who
could argue that they are not? They were the core
values of the Enron Corporation. Enron is best known
for an accounting fraud that sent it into bankruptcy in
2001 and cost many thousands of people their jobs,
investments and retirement funds. By now you
should be able to identify these values as relative
values. Relative values can easily become immoral
without respect for the Life Value of self and all
others as the basic premise that qualifies them. In the
Enron case, these seemly great moral values were
perverted. It started at the top and permeated the
entire company. The British actor and songwriter,
Noel Coward, once said, "The higher the buildings,
the lower the morals." Enron was a big company that

caused big problems. But you don't really have to be big to do great damage. Bernard Madoff's small investment company caused big problems, too. By the way, Madoff's hallmark values were: "value, fair-dealing, and high ethical standards."

Like you, I am aware of the many scandals involving business executives, elected officials and appointed civic leaders. The selfishness and immoral behavior exhibited by many of them is very troubling. The result has been a lack of trust in civic institutions, government, corporations and even the marketplace itself. Shameful reports of greed and corruption are in the newspapers every day, it seems. You would think that our leaders would know this and take care to avoid immoral behavior—especially in this age of instant media.

My perspectives also come from my experience as a businessman who has spent more than 25 years in the areas of information technology and business process outsourcing in healthcare and other industries. I am aware, in some depth, of the unethical practices of many large—and small—companies. It is very disturbing and disheartening. Where is an adherence to the Life Value? As a sales professional, I often go to trade shows and listen to the keynote speakers. From time to time I *am* the keynote speaker. I hear the "E - ethics" word thrown around a lot lately. Also the "T - trust" word. This is a good thing, of course. Any move to address this issue of ethics and trust is to be welcomed.

Unfortunately, many of our leaders are selfish—and accomplished ethical relativists. Let's face it, in order to get to the top in a dog-eat-dog world it sometimes helps to be the biggest, meanest dog. There are people, lacking in a balanced respect for self and others, who will do very unethical things to get ahead. Some have neither a conscience nor regard for others, except for how those others can be used to further their own goals. Let's not be naïve, such people exist, and too many rise to high positions because they are willing to do things that those of us of good conscience would not consider. Certainly you can become famous, and even rich, by doing good things for others in a very moral way. However, the things that can take you to the top in this world are just as easily skewed toward the self as toward others. You don't have to be a sociopath to have ethical issues. Some "regular" people with a conscience feel guilty about their own immoral behavior deep inside, but rationalize away their ethical lapses out of greed, hubris or fear—in other words, their emotions. A lifetime of exposure to ethical relativism doesn't help. "Everybody else is doing it..." Without first calibrating the old moral compass, it is easy to go wrong. This requirement applies to all of us, not just the sociopaths. So, what do we do? As we now know, any discussion of what to do about ethical problems of the world must transcend the context of relative values. Yet, cultural and environmental factors do have to be addressed objectively.

So, let's acknowledge the 800 pound gorilla in the room: money. We all need it; we all want it. For most of us, that means work, and work means a job. My active duty Marine Corps career was a small fraction of my life. Even with daily martial arts training, I have spent most of my adult life...working. Like most of you, I struggle in the marketplace every day and worry about it on weekends. Why? Because I need to make money. Along the way I have run into some pretty unethical people who think that they are ethical; and I have been called unethical by people who just didn't like what I did or how I went about doing it. Me! Unethical? It seemed so to them. Not to me, though. But, it felt bad just to be *called* unethical. Haven't most of us with a conscience had this kind of uncomfortable feeling?

If you are in business, you know it can be tough. Corporations can be hard on individuality. Bosses can be mean or inconsistent, downright cruel and plain old human (we never really hear much about the good bosses). Chuck Zamora, a corporate trainer and personal friend, has said that "people rarely quit jobs; they quit bosses." Why? Because they are disrespectful and unethical. Dissecting the current corporate culture—what is good with it and what is bad with it—is beyond the scope of this book. But, within the scope of our discussion is the ethical approach to having a job, working in a company (perhaps full of non-warriors, although that certainly doesn't make them bad people), and dealing with the trials and tribulations of the marketplace.

If ethics is moral, life-respecting behavior toward self and others—then *who* are the others? Logically, it has to be *all* others. As we have said repeatedly, this perspective is not easy for our tribally-oriented brains, but there is no other logical alternative—or life would be a relative value. Will I concede that the value of my life has a relative worth based upon what someone else thinks? Will you? No, my life is absolutely of equal worth to yours and vice versa, as the American Founding Fathers asserted.

When applying the Life Value concept to your business or professional life, remember one thing: your business must be respectful of self and all others. Who are the "all others?" They are your employees if you are a boss; your bosses and fellow employees if you are not the top boss. But the "all others" must necessarily include your customers, vendors, and...competitors. That last one is a hard one for many of us. Particularly if we feel that our competitors don't always play fair. Here is the $64 million question: Is being a "protector" in business— specifically, behaving respectfully and morally when dealing with competitors—naïve and dangerous? Does it make you tactically vulnerable to "cut-throats" and unethical competitors? Answer? Maybe. Being ethical can be risky, even perilous—so you better be good at what you do! However, in my experience, moral behavior pays off in the long run— both financially and psychologically. Remember, people like working with ethical people. But, again, you have to provide superior value to the customer. Many people will go out of their way to buy from people they respect—even if it costs a little more—rather than deal with business people perceived as disrespectful. I know I do.

Being respectful to others does not mean that you have to be tolerant of values and actions that are not contributing to the success and integrity of the business—that's moral and ethical relativism. There is no place for those in business. The values or work ethic of an individual or group can certainly be unacceptable or illegal. "All men are created equal." But that means their lives are equal; their cultures and behaviors—and job performance—can vary greatly. However, even if the behavior of an employee or competitor is unacceptable, here is my advice based upon experience: stick to the Life Value perspective and show respect for that person anyway. Deal respectfully with differences, address attitude and behavior issues objectively, even if it means you have to fire someone—or blow the whistle on them—and do what is ultimately in the best interests of self and others to the best of your ability. It is a better way, but it takes courage. Some training in moral courage and self-confidence may help. How about the martial arts? You rarely have to worry about fisticuffs in business, but having some martial training, in my experience, gives everyone more confidence—not only in fights, but also in life and at work.

As a Marine, I was exposed to many great leaders. As a civilian, I am sorry to say that I have had few. I remember one particular boss who was a real leader; but he didn't last long, as his bosses and the company's overall practices were often unethical. He wouldn't put up with it and quietly left.

One of the reasons I believe there were so many leaders in the Marines is two-fold: First, we were *trained* to be leaders. A great leader and 29th Commandant of the Marine Corps, General Alfred Gray, who I briefly served under in Korea, was said to have quipped, "If you see two Marines walking down the street, one of them is leading the other."

The other reason is that Marines, for the most part, are very physical, and they share adversity. Ethics are moral-physical and ethical leaders inspire trust. Would you want to follow a leader you didn't trust— or who didn't set the example? Marines often say, "Never ask someone to do something that you wouldn't do." What makes a good leader? The Marines have identified 14 leadership traits:

Judgment	Endurance
Justice	Bearing
Dependability	Unselfishness
Integrity	Courage
Decisiveness	Knowledge
Tact	Loyalty
Initiative	Enthusiasm

As you read through the list, you realize that there is no reason to memorize them;[39] you probably know them very well—and you can feel when a leader lacks one of these traits.

Would you like to be a good leader? Here are the 11 USMC leadership principles:

1. Know yourself and seek self-improvement.
2. Be technically and tactically proficient.
3. Develop a sense of responsibility among your subordinates.
4. Make sound and timely decisions.
5. Set the example.
6. Know your Marines and look out for their welfare.
7. Keep your Marines informed.
8. Seek responsibility and take responsibility for your actions.
9. Ensure assigned tasks are understood, supervised, and accomplished.
10. Train your Marines as a team.
11. Employ your command in accordance with its capabilities.

Like the Marine Corps' core values, the leadership principles are wonderfully universal. If you are not a Marine, you can still adapt them to your profession or situation. Practice them and you will become a better

---

[39] Although you could; the acronym is JJDIDTIEBUCKLE.

leader than you are today—maybe a *great* leader. But, remember, they are relative. The Life Value underpins all of these traits and principles. Go back; read them again. Without the Life Value of self and others as the foundational premise, they could all be used for very unethical purposes. Couldn't a drug lord exhibit many of these same traits and utilize these same principles to run a cocaine or heroin cartel? To a sociopathic leader, life is a relative value and the only well-being that he or she is concerned with is his or her own and that of *some* others. That some others could—and often does—change on a whim. Consider this quote: "We had no complaints," she said. "When [we] were in New York, for example, Papa gave a personal order to give us some money so we could run around the local boutiques."

Can you guess the identity of this generous boss "Papa" (who also gave his employees gold watches every year with his face on them)? It was Libyan leader Moammar Gadhafi.

Good and great leaders know that the "others" means *all* others, if possible. That is the crux of the largely unexamined Life Value that underpins all of the great values, traits and principles. The point of this book *is* to examine the Life Value, because we know that relying only on relative values, no matter how "great" or "moral" they may seem, is not enough. Seek the best balance of concern for self and all others, then apply the principles and seek to exemplify the traits above and I know you will do good—and also well.

I spoke before a group of business leaders in Tokyo after the 2011 tsunami which knocked out a large percentage of the nuclear power in the country. A frightening amount of radioactivity was released into the sea, air and water supply. A very important issue that was buried within the larger scope of the tragedy was the behavior of some "leaders" who had the resources to protect themselves and their families and did so, abandoning their employees to face the catastrophe without support. Particularly acute were the hard feelings toward foreign business leaders who fled (remember, it is even easier to demonize those outside your ethnic or cultural "in-group"). The Japanese word for "foreigner" is *gaijin*. Those foreign businessmen were called *"fly-jin"* for how they flew away and left their employees behind.

So, we can see that failures of ethical leadership have international implications and require objective communication that leaves dehumanizating and demonizing words out of the dialogue.

Leaders must be ethical; that is the foundation. They must also be able to communicate effectively and respectfully, under duress and across cultural divides if necessary. That's where the cultural detective skills in Chapter 5 come in to play. Leaders must also have certain important skills, especially *courage*—both moral and physical.

We used the graphic on the next page to frame the topic.

Figure 11 – The Leadership Pyramid

Because Japan is the home of the samurai warrior, known for both honor and courage, the concept of a Life Value of self and others resonated with most everyone. Not coincidentally, the word samurai comes from the Japanese word *sabauru*, which means "to serve."

Many of us in leadership positions strive to be effective and ethical. There are many books and training opportunities available focused toward that end. I have read many of them and conclude that the Dual Life Value concept, clarified and activated—including a sustainment plan for practicing ethical behavior—has been the insufficiently articulated missing piece.

I once had a boss who was extremely disrespectful to an employee in a meeting. That employee happened to report to me. When we went back to our office the employee was very discouraged and depressed. Actually, he was crying. The big boss called me a bit later and asked me how I thought the meeting went. I was truthful and said that his behavior and remarks had upset this employee, so I didn't think the meeting went well at all. He bellowed, "Oh yeah? Well you both get over here." Uh oh. So we both had to go back over to his office. The boss sat us both down and confronted the employee, saying something like, "Jack tells me you think the meeting wasn't very motivating." The employee, scared out of his wits, avoided my eyes, looked up at the boss and said..."No, I think the meeting went great."

I learned a valuable lesson. When dealing with unethical and disrespectful people on someone else's behalf, as in this case, your job is not to attack the boss, but to *protect the employee*. I was not wrong to want to tell the boss that he had been out of line, but I was wrong to put my employee in such a defenseless position. It would have been better to comfort the employee and find a different way to deal with the boss. That would have been the better short-term approach.

I eventually left that job, started my own company, and have never been happier. That was the long-term solution. I knew I was unhappy at that old job, but the stress and fear that I was operating under wasn't fully apparent until I left. The "caught in the middle" feeling is another one of those Life Value conundrums; you want to protect yourself and you want to protect others, but it is sometimes a no-win situation. It is probably better if you protect others over yourself. Yes, it may be more dangerous for you, but you end up with that magic feeling of nobility which is, perhaps, the most satisfying of all human feelings. It is the intangible reward for living as an Ethical Warrior. It is a better life.

So, what if you are not in a leadership position—yet? Often, as followers or employees or plain old citizens, we are confronted with ethical deficiencies in our leaders that we feel powerless to address without getting ourselves in trouble or fired. Sometimes we have to leave a job that pressures us to be unethical and/or participate in unethical corporate behaviors, particularly if we are dealing with a sociopathic boss. That takes...courage. But not all bad bosses are sociopaths. Some just don't have a reliable moral compass that functions well under stress. You might be able to help them.

The best way to help them is to model ethical behavior yourself, and inspire them with your own words and actions—and sometimes a little cleverness.

The King, Bazgul and the Innkeeper

Have you ever heard the story of Bazgul Badakhshi? He was a very famous Afghan folk musician who lived to the age of 105. When Afghanistan was still ruled by a King,

Bazgul was invited to the capital, Kabul, to perform at the palace. Bazgul was not a rich man; he had no money to pay for a hotel after a long trip from the north. He was not worried, however, because he had been promised a respectable fee for his performance. He arrived in Kabul the night before he was to sing and checked in to a modest hotel, telling the proprietor why he was there, and that he would pay his hotel bill as soon as he was paid by the king.

The next day he performed marvelously, so beautifully, in fact, that the King was overcome by his emotions and forgot to pay Bazgul his fee! Bazgul fretfully went back to the hotel with the bad news. The hotel owner threatened to have Bazgul arrested. But Bazgul had an idea on how to get the money. He shared the plan with the innkeeper who agreed to play his part.

Every day the King would tour the capital in his automobile so that he would be visible to his people. He always took the same route, and that route went right by the hotel where Bazgul was staying.

Sure enough, the next morning the King's car headed down the street toward the inn right on time. As planned, the innkeeper chased Bazgul out of the hotel in front of the King's car, beating the singer about the head and shoulders with a broom yelling: "This man is a thief and a liar!"

The King recognized the man being beaten as Bazgul and had his driver stop the car. The King got out and demanded to know why the innkeeper was beating the beloved singer. The innkeeper repeated that the man was a thief and a liar. The King demanded that the innkeeper explain himself.

"Well, this man stayed at my hotel last night and didn't pay, so he is a thief," said the innkeeper."

"But why is he a liar?" asked the King.

"He is a liar because he told me that he sang for the King last night, and the King did not pay him. Well, that is a lie; because we have only one King in this country and that King is honorable and would never fail to pay a debt!"

The King realized his omission of the night before, was chagrined, paid Bazgul—and the hotel owner—and everyone was happy.

Just as Bazgul helped the King act ethically, we can sometimes do the same thing, but it may require us to be as clever. Say that you uncover padded sales results; you might say something like "I reviewed the sales report and I think we have an error. I know you [the boss] demand honesty and accuracy in our department, so it looks like we will have to change the numbers to reflect lower sales and strive to do better next month." Few non-sociopaths would be able to resist that kind of leadership from below. In fact, many would be grateful for the reminder because they want to be ethical, too.

However, you can't expect to always be able to handle unethical situations in the workplace easily. You have to be ready (practiced), and cool under stress—and able to face the consequences, *regardless of what they are*, with courage, honor and grace. Those consequences may include being overlooked for a promotion, getting fired, or having to quit. But, have courage and keep to the high road. The bottom line is that ethics *is* the bottom line in all great businesses, and it is bound to pay off in the long run—even if only in terms of your own serenity and long-term happiness. But, remember, you have to be good!

Chapter 8
Activating the Ethic

"A person educated in mind and not in morals is a
menace to society."
- *Juanita Kidd Stout*

"Everybody is a genius. But if you judge a fish by its
ability to climb a tree, it will live its whole life
believing that it is stupid."
- *Albert Einstein*

"Music is the universal language of mankind."
- *Henry Wadsworth Longfellow*

"Dad, school is a jail for kids."
- *Danny Hoban, 7 years old*

I don't think of myself as a teacher, but I do teach
a lot. I have found that there are several important
points regarding the Life Value and the nature of
human nature that pertain to education and learning
that calls for deeper discussion. In the course of
training Marines, we have come to understand that
moral values are best transmitted and learned
through an "activation process" that utilizes:

- A story with emotional impact—especially if it
  is true rather than a myth, fable or legend, etc.

211

- A "teachable moment" that occurs in context of an event that has moral import.
- Shared adversity.

What about "school learning?" Can a better understanding of our human nature help us to learn more effectively? Is an understanding of the Life Value important in education?

Knowledge and learning are inherently valuable to self and others. This is obvious but warrants overt acknowledgement. People have different aptitudes for different kinds of learning. We are a long way from completely understanding how humans learn best. Since Daniel Goldman's book, Emotional Intelligence,[40] we are now aware that emotional abilities may be just as important as—or more important than—raw intelligence for a happier, more successful, yet balanced life. Intellectual and emotional intelligence are both important for learning. I have done much training and teaching and, in my experience, people learn best when they are *both* emotionally engaged and physically stimulated. This formula works for everybody, not just people who are committed and excited to learn. Unfortunately, many people are not committed and excited to learn. They include our children. Kids don't like school.[41] This is not good. Children who

---

[40] Goldman, D., Emotional Intelligence: Why It Can Matter More Than IQ, 1996.

[41] Why Don't Students Like School: A Cognitive Scientist Answers Questions About How the Mind Works and What It Means for the Classroom. Daniel T. Willingham, Jossey-Bass; 1 edition (March 15, 2010).

genuinely like and look forward to typical school learning are few and far between, in my experience. Kids are natural learners (watch them figure out amazingly complicated video games), but when it comes to school it seems like their minds are turned off. There are, of course, exceptions to this and there may be many schools that have discovered the secret to learning, but they are by far the minority. Many kids whom I know claim to hate (OK, dislike) school. What can be done?

Humphrey, with help from his sons, in a project sponsored by National University in San Diego, successfully educated "uneducable" gang kids in southern California on the border with Mexico. His experimental high school utilized a balanced moral-mental-artistic-physical program based on the Life Value. He literally pulled gang kids off the streets with the enticement that he would teach them how to box if they attended his school. It worked. I know because I was there. These tough gang members, kicked out of every school that they had ever attended, were learning with incredible joy—and speed—at the Life Values School. They were highly competent scholastically, regardless of their "IQ," and they were very socially engaged; any one of them would get up in front of the class and sing a song at any time without fear or embarrassment. The Life Values School had a much higher graduation rate than the local public high schools. Nearly 30 years later, I still correspond with one of the students. He is currently a Sergeant Major in the Marines.

People asked how the Life Value could possibly be activated in these semi-insane gang-members, often heavy drug users, who were slobbering with hate and who might kill for a pair of sneakers—or nothing at all. Humphrey would say that they were the same as anybody else in terms of "self and others." "Don't even dare look at one of their gang members unkindly. Unfortunately, the entire species for them is limited to their own families and their own gangs."

Humphrey said that these kids believed that they had been relegated to outlaw status through savagely unequal public schools and racism. "The violence was a political statement. All we had to do in order to stop violence by hard-core, young, criminal dropouts was the same thing we did in the volatile overseas Cold-War arena: Inspire them to expand the boundaries of the species-protecting Life Value outside of their arbitrarily defined in-group. With the knowledge of how human values are taught, we found we could bring these seemingly outcast kids into a mutually respectful and productive classroom setting, even when there previously had been constant violence."

I was introduced to Humphrey's unusual educational approach in a way that will certainly sound odd—perhaps shocking—to most modern day parents and educators. He asked me to come in and teach a gym class on...knife fighting. Actually it was on defense against a knife attack. Can you imagine teaching anything at all to do with knife fighting skills in a high school today? The fact is that frightened youth will tend to carry knives and guns, even though carrying weapons is usually more dangerous than not being armed—that is, more dangerous to them! One of the ways we used to help these kids overcome the distracting fear they felt living in their tough neighborhoods was to teach them how to defend themselves against knives. They needed to know this more than they needed to learn badminton (which was "taught" in my son's middle school gym class). So that's what we did; we gave them physical self-confidence so that they could address their real concerns (fear), and then concentrate on their studies. Once they got a certain amount of confidence, they stopped carrying knives themselves.

Humphrey and his sons ran schools for dropouts not only in San Diego, but on Indian Reservations in Canada, as well as in schools for at-risk teens in two other major U.S. cities. They found that they could never beat the negative drug and violence problems in teenagers simply with direct attacks on those behaviors. *They had to show them something better.* Change required a strong, positive and inspiring program based on the Life Value. Teachers *had* to set the example—as physical, as well as, ethical and intellectual role models. If they were smokers, they had to give up the cigarettes. If they were not fit, they had to make a sincere effort to become so. Teachers were called Role Model Educational Guardians—and they had to be.

Along with the usual reading, writing and arithmetic, the curriculum included other human natural pursuits like music, art and general physical fitness. It was necessarily a *total person* approach to education. *There* is where the success is found, and consequently, greater happiness, too. With a good, busy, positive program, the problems could, to a considerable degree, be ignored; the negative issues tended to be superseded by the positive and wither away.

And it had to include martial arts. When I first met Humphrey, he and his sons were using a modified version of boxing that they called STRIKE. I still use it today with my martial arts students.

STRIKE is fun, exciting, a little scary, but extremely safe. Briefly, we have found that we can quickly and easily teach young men and women necessary close-in, sustained "fire in the face" fear-and-stress-control through these two exercises:

1. **STRIKE Training.** To teach the students to overcome fear, we have trusted sparring partners, called "catchers," do light sparring with the students. It is a real stress-control lesson, particularly for those who have never been in a physical conflict. The student is coached until he or she learns to hit confidently at the experienced catchers. A rope is placed between the "student" and the catcher. At any point, if the "student" feels overwhelmed or just needs a break, he or she can step back away from the rope and the catcher will not follow. The catchers defend themselves by

slipping punches, bobbing, weaving, and (at least initially) only jabbing back toward the face of the student. As the student becomes more proficient (and often more aggressive), the catcher starts to throw light jabs to the face as needed to help the hitter learn to control his or her emotions "under fire." Just this small amount of light sparring can provide enough fear, minimal pain and stress for the student to experience the feeling of passing successfully through fear to appropriate action. As the student gains confidence and begins to hit harder and with more accuracy, the catcher then throws more and quicker jabs until the student is, again, feeling overwhelmed. This process repeats—raise the confidence, raise the stress, raise the confidence, raise the stress— until the student can successfully overcome the stress of the close-in hitting and hit back with some reasonable degree of efficacy.

In STRIKE training, many first-timers, when confronted with a gloved opponent, will behave in a totally irrational manner: the learner will cover up and offer zero offense, or even turn away from the "threat" despite a friendly instructor and assurances that they won't be aggressively attacked. In spite of the natural Life Value inclination to preserve their own life, they fail to protect themselves; it can be *that* stressful. It is also philosophically interesting to note that *some* first timers act in the opposite manner, but again, in contradiction to the Life Value: they attack with vehemence attempting to *really* knock their friendly instructor senseless. In the process, the aggressive beginner is laughably open to attack, and invariably totally winded and helpless, in 30 to 45 seconds. It does not take long to correct either misfire; the physical program is amazingly effective, and the psychological/ethical lessons are sublime.

Two important notes regarding the catcher: (1) the catcher must be skilled and experienced enough to protect himself or herself against an average opponent (do *not* put two inexperienced fighters together; this is a sure recipe for serious injuries); and, (2) The catcher must also be of high moral character (and good-natured enough) to absorb the "lucky" punch without getting angry and wanting to get even.

2. **Hitting Training.** To gain confidence, the students are first taught straight, untelegraphed (meaning the punch is not pulled back or "chambered"), relaxed, heavy hitting on bags with fists, palms, claw-hands and elbows. The three secrets to superior hitting are:

a. With a relaxed hand and arm cocked in the boxer's hitting position, start your punch with a slight forward movement of the head while starting up onto the toes of the rear foot as the beginning of your untelegraphed punch. That punch is a twist-explosion of the entire hitting side of your body behind a relaxed catapulting fist (or extended fingers).

b. An instant after the fist (relaxed but with a firm wrist) deep-smacks into the target with the puncher's weight behind it, retract the arm into its cocked, face-protecting position.

c. Your hands and head (with chin down) should not move too far off center, (even if a boxer teaches you to "hook"). You should be able to follow any blow with the other hand as in a 1, 2, 1, 2 continuous sequences without losing your balance.

Straight punches are enough. Well practiced, any man, woman, or adolescent can land that blow with a fist into the neck, or fingers into the eyes, of an unsuspecting attacker. It will be adequately disconcerting to allow for a running escape or for a follow-up as necessary. Humphrey and I agreed that students should be encouraged to enroll in a martial arts or wrestling program for a foundation in grappling. Tactical movement skills, like those we teach to Marines and law enforcement officers, are also important (the maneuver skills needed for tactical combatives is quite different than those of sport martial arts).

Why is physical unarmed fighting ability needed by modern civilian teenagers in order to learn to be ethical? The answer is: because, moral action tends to encounter opposition. The problems range from fear of bullies, through fear of saying no to drug salesmen, through the temptation to act unethically to keep a job or maintain a relationship, and on and on, to fear of stopping international genocide. If we are afraid, it is very hard to say no to bad things and bad people. An inability to fight may also contribute to fear and prevent moral action.

Humphrey, in private correspondence, wrote: "We are still physical animals to the degree that we need to be able to fight to feel like 'family-protectors.' That is what we have been in our small communities all through history. This need to understand fighting is why men will pay more to see the top world-championship fight than for any other activity in the world. A young man's need to know how to fight showed up overwhelmingly in all of our attitude studies among dropouts in San Diego and among our troops in Turkey, Korea, Okinawa and Vietnam, as well as on several ships at sea. Without the physical fighting ability, along with the constructive moral education, many will often try to prove their manhood to themselves and others through a phony toughness. This includes incessant vulgarity, heavy drinking, swaggering, bullying and beating women.

Historically, it manifested itself as atrocities in combat, such as cutting off ears of the injured and tromping gold teeth from the mouths of the dead."

By teaching men "true toughness" with (1) unarmed fighting skills, and (2) the knowledge of the noble feelings that come from a readiness to protect others, we can upgrade our confused teenagers, en masse, to the moral status that they would like to possess: that of young moral giants—protectors of the innocent.

As an historical note, the STRIKE program when utilized in the Humphrey's Life Values School was originally intended to target the male gang members. While the boys were to engage in STRIKE, the girls were to participate in a high quality aerobics/dance class. The girls wanted the popular dance class, but *demanded* the STRIKE training, too. Several of the girls expressed their fear of attack and a lack of confidence in protectors coming to their aid. The girls (many also gang-affiliated) were better students of STRIKE than the boys. Humphrey found the same to be true in Canada, among native Cree students.

I even saw Humphrey use the protection skills to reach and inspire a tough gang member, quickly and spontaneously, in a store.

Shopping Trip in the Central Valley

I was with Bob Humphrey in Stockton, California, in an area known for quite violent Hispanic and Asian gangs. We were being stalked by this aggressive gangbanger in a sporting goods store. I could almost hear his thoughts: "What are you white people doing in here?"

The guy looked like a problem, so I prepared myself for a confrontation and maybe a fight. But it was Bob who approached him. "Hey, do you know how to box?" "Huh?" The kid said. And, before you know it, Bob, probably in his mid-60s, was teaching him how to box using a heavy bag hanging in the store.

The gangbanger asked, "Like this?" And Humphrey coaching him said, "Get your elbow in there!" "Keep on your toes!" Bob was tough, his instruction exacting, and the kid loved it! I couldn't believe it. The kid had expressed such overt hostility for outsiders initially, but in a short period of time he and Bob were like old friends. This kid was totally turned around! Then Bob put his arm over his shoulder and told him to only use his "new" hitting skills to protect others. The guy smiled and was thanking Bob by the time we left.

Unbelievable—from thug to protector in about 10 minutes.

Most young men (and women) I work with are delighted to become morally and physically competent as a protector because a thirst for the feeling of human nobility is in their guts. I have also seen moral/physical education cure confirmed racists. Once they see others as equals, and gain the noble feeling of being a protector, they become the strongest defenders of the previously hated groups.

The final piece of Humphrey's educational approach revolved around mental and artistic skills. When Humphrey's group (mainly he and his sons) were working with the high-school dropouts, they found that the problem wasn't only a lack of physical self-confidence; there was also a great deal of intellectual insecurity. The kids thought that they couldn't be educated because they had always been treated as if they were not smart. It was a chicken and egg, vicious circle, situation. They felt stupid because they were uneducated and they felt that education was useless because they were stupid. Many would have deemed the situation hopeless, but not Bob Humphrey.

After arriving at an agreement with the students' mothers and the police, the Humphreys forced the late night, drug-abusing gang-members to come to school. They did their own truancy; disarmed the youth and forced them to stay in class. Once at school, participating in the Life Values curriculum, most were easy to work with; it was getting them out of bed and out the door that was a problem. Sound familiar? It is the same with most teenagers everywhere (including mine).

For the first month, each day and each hour was a struggle of winning or losing everything. The STRIKE training, plus singing, and other forms of artistic expression—teachers doing soft-shoes competitions, for example—kept the kids engaged. The Humphreys used anything morally acceptable they could think of to keep those angry, cynical youth entertained, challenged and in the classroom. Of course, that was only "a temporary fix."

In those times (and these), education often seems so horribly boring and irrelevant that the kids start to think there is something wrong with *them*. I once received a call from my son's second grade teacher on a Friday night. She was very upset because my son had treated her disdainfully. (Disdainfully? A seven year old?) I asked my son about it and he looked me in the eye and uttered a statement that floored me. He said, very matter-of-factly, but with an undercurrent of misery, "Dad, school is a jail for kids." This is what we are dealing with in education today.

The Humphreys knew that they had to find something extra special to convince dropouts that school was worthwhile and also prove to them that they were intelligent enough to succeed. The Humphreys had addressed the moral element with the Life Value concept; they had addressed the physical confidence with the STRIKE training and robust physical fitness classes, but they also speculated that there might be some such special key to better, faster mental education. They found it.

It was the overlooked ancient Greek discovery of fast learning through imagery. For textbooks, they used Harry Lorayne's books on this confidence-raising ability.[42] The imagery-learning ability, like the Life Value and the life-protecting fighting ability, tapped right into the kids' human nature. You just had to teach it correctly—synergistically.

"Imagery learning" involves the so-called artistic right brain. Its usefulness for the academic recovery of dropouts and troubled students is truly astonishing. I personally witnessed Humphrey's students confound college professors with their ability to memorize lists of dates, facts and even random lists of words, with their amazing memory skills. I could also see the quiet pride and confidence on the students' faces.

That general topic of the right-artistic brain, and *art* in its broadest meaning, excited Humphrey almost as much as the moral and physical training. It, too, was an ideal tool to help keep children in the otherwise boring schools. The kids sang, told stories, drew pictures, danced and listened to music in class. They loved all of it. It was in their nature.

The interesting thing is that the arts are equally good for foreign peacemaking assignments. The artistic skills are perfect for winning over the people, socially, in the streets, villages and jungles of the world. My ability to sing a little bit and play the guitar has been invaluable to me in my life—both at home and around the world. I have played Christmas songs in the Philippines, folk songs in Ireland, bossa novas in South America, karaoke in Japan, blues in

---

[42] The Memory Book: The Classic Guide to Improving Your Memory at Work, at School, and at Play. Lorayne, H. and Lucas, J. 1974.

Slovenia, and been the only white person in a gospel-singing black Baptist church in the south. I've never had a serious problem. Music is that close to the core of our human nature and it reminds us that we are clearly more the same than different.

You may be wondering whatever happened to Humphrey's schools. They were eventually all closed by the "establishment." Why? The short answer is that they may have been "too successful," and an unacceptable challenge to the status quo. After all, if Humphrey could graduate 90% of his gangsters, why were the fully funded public schools in the same districts full of "normal" kids only graduating 60%? This is an example of the common "Kill Socrates" syndrome that we will discuss in the Afterword. One of the most successful schools in America is Naperville Central High School in Naperville, Illinois. It is featured in my friend John Ratey's book "Spark"[43] as a model of how exercise and academics can reinforce each other for both superior scholastic results and good health. Naperville Central's synergistic fitness and academic program has been so successful that Paul Zientarski, the retired physical education coordinator who championed it, now spends his time touring the country teaching other schools how they did it. In a private meeting I asked him how he likes travelling so much. He told me he felt he had no choice because no one in his local area

---

[43] Ratey M.D, John J., Spark: The Revolutionary New Science of Exercise and the Brain, 2008

would listen to him. I was shocked. He laughed and said, "I can't even get the other high schools in our own school district to try the approach." "Why?" I asked incredulously. "Politics, jealousy, you know..." Can you believe it? Relative values superseding the Life Value once again—to the detriment of millions of "jailed" school kids.

By the way, when I asked Paul specifically whether he felt that ethics should be part of the formula and if physical exercise could enhance values training, he said that he had never really thought about it. Later in the conversation, he told me about a mentoring program that the school had implemented to pair accomplished student athletes with struggling kids. The idea was to help the mentees flourish in high school and also discourage bullying. I laughed and said that I thought the mentors were budding Ethical Warriors and that he was including the moral element, but was just taking it for granted. Do you see why I keep saying that we shouldn't overlook the step of clarifying the Life Value in everything we do? Let's *not* take it for granted!

PART II

The Ethical Warrior

Chapter 9
Sustaining the Ethic

"He who fights with monsters should be careful lest
he thereby become a monster."
- *Friedrich Nietzsche*

"After many months of 'no worse enemy'...we are
very pleased to seize opportunities to demonstrate 'no
better friend.'"
- *General Joe Dunford, USMC*

As a young Marine Captain, just off the drill field
at the Recruit Depot in San Diego, I decided to earn a
Master's Degree at night. You know that I met my
mentor, Robert Humphrey, at that time; he was one of
my professors.

During this period of my life, I thought of myself
as a tough guy. I would walk around town with a
scowl on my face, challenging everyone I met with
my eyes. Those of you who have had some martial
arts training—have you ever fantasized about using
it? That was me. I would walk into a bar or
restaurant, look around, then mentally destroy
everyone in the place before I could relax, sit down
and order a meal or have a beer.

My aggressive attitude must have finally irritated
Humphrey because he eventually took me aside and

said: "Jack, I have to ask, do you realize that you make people very uncomfortable? You have a way of challenging everyone you meet." I shrugged, but inside I was secretly pleased, as in "well they *should* be uncomfortable, because I am such a 'badass'!" Humphrey could see that I wasn't getting it. But he was patient and smart. Rather than telling me I was a fool, he gave me some extra homework. He said, "Jack, tonight when you go out, instead of looking at everyone like you want to intimidate them, try this instead, say to yourself: 'everyone in this place is a little *safer* because I am here.'"

I respected Humphrey very much by this time, so I decided to try his suggestion. I often went to a place in Ocean Beach called the Red Garter. It was like the Star Wars bar—full of tough guys (and gals), personnel from the various military services, bikers, Soviet spies (this was during the Cold War) and plenty of trouble if you wanted it. But this time, instead of acting like my usual confrontational self, I stopped in the doorway, surveyed the scene and said to myself: "Everyone in this place is a little safer because I am here; anyone in need has at least one friend because of me and my skills."

Well everybody ignored me, of course, and nothing happened on the outside. But on the inside— well, even as I write this, I get that tingly feeling on my face and scalp. As I stood there, virtually unnoticed by everyone else at the Red Garter, I had one of those life-changing epiphanies. I realized, WOW, that felt a LOT better than what I was doing!

That lesson in context changed my life and maybe even saved it. It turned me from a self-styled "badboy" into a protector; and I continue to recommend it to my audiences all over the world. I invite you to try it yourself, today:

Wherever I go, everyone is a little safer because I am there.

By the way, Humphrey's lessons on warriorship weren't over by a long shot. If you want to hear a *really* embarrassing story that happened 16 years later, keep reading.

It must be clear by now that I was inspired to adopt the Life Value of protecting self and all others because I was exposed to the code of the Ethical Warrior by two mentors: Bob Humphrey and my Japanese teacher Masaaki Hatsumi. Hatsumi Sensei, especially, has been my martial arts inspiration for nearly 30 years and his example greatly informs my grasp of the Life Value. It bears repeating, however, that this book isn't necessarily for warriors; the lessons are accessible and applicable to anyone who wants to live ethically. Warrior lessons can clarify the complex topic of values, morals and ethics and help them come alive for just about everybody. The reason is that virtually all of us—not just warriors—have the Life Value. We just "get it." Where did we get this Life Value from? Nature, nurture, implanted by God, all of the above? It doesn't really matter–it just is. "A is A." That's how we know it is right; it is part of our human nature. It is self-evident to the extent that when we encounter individuals who *don't* have it (i.e. sociopaths who have an abnormally low "others" value; or suicides who have an abnormally low "self" value) it is perfectly obvious to virtually all of us. We are also natural protectors. Think about it, aren't there certain people who you would protect—perhaps at risk of your own life? Can you think of a stronger imperative? It may be true that, during most of our days, the life and death sense of immediacy one feels in combat doesn't exist. But the organic balancing mechanism that bids us to protect self and others is always operating. In war, the Life Value is just more starkly apparent. Even if we are not "warriors," a better understanding of the Life Value can still inform our value systems and how we prioritize our relative values—especially if we activate it and practice it. So how does the concept of an Ethical Warrior apply to everyday life? You will be able to connect the dots if you try. It's easy.

There have been many cycles of peace as well as war in human history. War was famously defined by Carl von Clausewitz as "the continuation of politics by other means." I don't know about you, but that definition is about as clear as mud to me. I would define war as a violent and physical clash of competing values. Often, the relative values of one group (typically the aggressor) are used to supersede the Life Value of another group. Whatever the definition, however, it seems as if war is a recurring inevitability.

If we are lucky, we may never have to fight in a war. For the most part that has been the case for me. So, I have spent most of my life training and using my *physical* protector skills only very rarely except in training. I often train military and police personnel, and they have used the skills that I have taught them in war and other violent situations, such as when they deal with violent criminals, etc. I have not been called to that degree. Most of the time I just go to work, come home to my family, and interact with my friends, neighbors and myriad strangers. Yet, after a lifetime of feeling inclined to be a protector, I feel compelled to keep my warrior skills sharp, so I train daily. I am not alone; there are many who have this strong inclination. They come from all walks of life— not just the military and law enforcement. They are the citizen warriors that rise to the occasion during emergencies and disasters—or just go out of their way to lend a hand, even when it is inconvenient, hard or dangerous. Maybe you are one of them. I believe that a warrior lives the Life Value regardless of his "day job." That is, he or she lives by the protector ethic on a daily basis in a very positive way.

If you have been a warrior, it is important that you reclaim your place as a functioning member of society when you return and reassume your position as a citizen warrior. For example, I have met many people in the Marine Corps who could not function well during the peace that followed the Vietnam War. Yes, they were fighters, as they had proven many times in combat; but they did not become well-adjusted civilians. They could barely function as peacetime Marines. That phenomenon has continued with the Iraq and Afghanistan wars as well. And, unfortunately, it isn't over.

One of my roles in the Marine Corps Martial Arts Program (MCMAP) is to address this issue of resiliency and psychological health with Marines before they go to war, and again after they return. This is one of the important aspects of the Ethical Warrior concept. In fact, we believe that MCMAP, as a physical-*moral* training regimen can inoculate Marines before the stress of combat and mediate the effects of Post-Traumatic Stress Disorder (PTSD) afterward. Unsurprisingly, the key value that we focus on is the Dual Life Value of self and all others. Understanding the implications of the "dehumanization" and "demonization" concepts is also vital for building resiliency to combat stress in our Marines.

In his book, "Achilles in Vietnam,"[44] Jonathan Shay discusses dehumanization and disrespect of the enemy as a prime cause of PTSD. The bottom line is that respect for the enemy as an equal human being— even though his behavioral values may be immoral— is essential in mitigating combat PTSD. Marine Corps core values—with the Life Value as the foundational, clarifying and qualifying value—charge Marines to act with honor, courage and commitment. But even

---

[44] Achilles in Vietnam, Simon & Schuster (October 1, 1995), by Jonathan Shay

more basic is a Marine's respect for all life—killing only when necessary to protect lives. Killing, even as a protector, is hard, but it can be ethical. And this approach avoids dehumanization of the enemy, thus mitigating to a certain extent the severity of PTSD and help avoid "moral injury." Moral injury is the psychological stress that results from performing violent acts on others without necessity or with a psychologically immoral perspective. According to Shay, there are at least two other prime reasons for PTSD. The first is the exposure to, or participation in, violence and killing. No surprise there. The second is...betrayal by one's leadership. You do this hard and dangerous thing in defense of others at extreme risk to yourself, and after it is over, you are abandoned by your leadership. Devastating. Welcome to the post-Vietnam experience for so many of our, now, middle aged veterans.

In contrast to a training methodology that includes "demonizing or dehumanization," consider the perspective described in the following points. Most are direct quotes from Israeli military snipers who served during the Al-Aqsa Intifada, a period of intensified Palestinian–Israeli violence which occurred between 2000 and 2005.[45]

- "The assumption that soldiers have to be distanced from their enemies, seen by scholars

---

[45] Israeli snipers in the Al-Aqsa intifada: killing, humanity and lived experience. Bar, Neta & Ben-Ari, Eyal. Third World Quarterly, Vol 26. No. 1, pp 133-152, 2005

as being indispensable for killing, is not wholly vindicated in our case."

- "If you don't see the enemy as a human being, you really become a war machine. You lose your humanity if you don't think about him as human."
- "I don't know what to tell you, every human being is a human being. I see many Arabs here and I don't hate any one of them. Each one has his own truth. I also don't want to kill any one of them. But the minute I see anyone go out to a terror attack, someone with a weapon comes to our area, I will shoot him without any guilt because that is the situation here in the country."
- "Snipers continue to do their work in a cool and calm manner out of a full belief in the justice of their cause. Indeed, the belief that they are preventing the next terror attack or suicide bomber is a key motivator for them."
- "For snipers the Palestinians they shoot are threatening human beings, threatening to them, to their fellow soldiers and (potentially) to Israeli civilians. Thus the assignation of 'terrorist' should not be understood as necessarily contradictory to their being humans. Terrorists, for the snipers, as for the majority of Israeli combat troops, do not belong to some category of evil non-human beings but are human beings who are perceived to be dangerous."

This surely gives a different perspective to the conventional wisdom, as well as scholarly consensus, that in order to kill morally soldiers have to dehumanize their enemies. The following is also from the same article and quotes Shay's book:

> "[The] Israeli situation stands in contrast to that of the US forces, which were characterised for long historical periods by an almost obligatory demonisation of enemies and their portrayal as the foes of civilisation. Fussel, Cameron, Dower, Eisenhart and Shatan all contend that enemies were demonised by the US military during World War II, Korea and the Vietnam War. Kennett suggests that, while the German soldier inspired no strong detestation, the strong animosity to Japanese soldiers was based on a combination of racism and religious legitimation. Twenty years later, as Shay remarks, the Vietnamese 'were thought of as monkeys, insects, vermin, childlike, unfeeling automata, puny…inscrutable, uniquely treacherous, deranged, physiologically inferior, primitive, barbaric and devoted to fanatical suicide charges'. Against this background, it is perhaps not surprising that American soldiers had the (unofficial) 'mere gook rule' which declared that killing a Vietnamese civilian did not really count."

And this, which pertains to betrayal by those who you are sworn to protect:

> "Within the context of contemporary Israel, marked as it is by a widespread consensus about the threat armed Palestinians pose, the killing is understood as normal, justified, clear and unquestionable. In fact, one could argue that, because the IDF [Israeli Defense Force] is very widely understood as necessary and trusted by Israeli Jews, the snipers are less traumatised."

A thorough understanding of the Dual Life Value would, I believe, have rendered these quotes unsurprising and predictable. They did for me when I read them.

Due to our all-volunteer armed forces, military service and the real prospects of war are an abstraction for most of us. These lessons from warriors may be something that we would neither encounter in our normal conversations nor experience ourselves. But, one technological advance brings millions of us closer...video games. Many people, especially teenagers, are captivated by, maybe addicted to, graphic video warrior games. I think it would be interesting to find out how many of these video games (if any) include the Ethical Warrior element. There is a great deal of discourse on the pros and cons of violent video games, so I'll leave it at that.

But, I wonder how many "martial art warriors" and "keyboard soldiers" really understand the sickness that can come from taking life. The sickness is even more assured when the fighting and killing is done from a relative or emotional perspective. No video game can prepare you for the real emotional aspects of war and killing.

Both Humphrey and Hatsumi taught that the purpose of martial arts is to *protect* life. This focus on the Life Value is key. I had the opportunity to introduce these men to each other at one point, and it was clear from discussions afterward that they were in complete agreement on the true purpose of warriorship. In fact, Hatsumi presented Humphrey with a posthumous 10th degree black belt after his death, which is a rare honor.

For Marines, the Life Value manifests itself as the Ethical Warrior concept. What is an Ethical Warrior?

An Ethical Warrior is a protector of life.
Whose life?
Self and Others?
Which Others?
All others, if possible,
Killing only when necessary to protect life.

I have learned in my thirty-plus years of martial arts training that the Ethical Warrior lifestyle is like an antidote to the sickness of killing another human being. Because the warrior must kill to protect life, the training can help protect the spirit of the warrior from succumbing to the sickness that comes from taking a life.

You may or may not be a Marine, but I believe the Ethical Warrior Concept is instructive for all of us. It pertains to an aspect of the human experience that is very clear, even if we often overlook it on a day-to-day basis. It is the matter of life and death. We have all experienced the stark reality of life and death at one time or another, perhaps as a result of a sudden passing of a relative or friend. Life is very delicate, and death can be a mere moment away. When we are confronted with it—even a natural death—we tend to re-prioritize. We gain, if only temporarily, a clearer perspective on what is truly important. Strong relative values suddenly don't seem so imperative. Life reveals itself clearly as the most important, superseding value. There exists a plethora of sayings, poems and bumper stickers devoted to the concept of getting one's priorities straight. Most of us have inspired flashes of re-prioritization in our lives. But even after a close up and personal encounter with death the feeling wears off rather quickly. Perhaps this is a good thing, but it often leads us back to the way we were before—back toward stress and the niggling unhappinesses that beset us when we again lose sight of the Life Value.

Those who have witnessed war—even those who have only been trained for war—can have an attuned sense of the Life Value, even if they have never had the concept philosophically clarified for them. My experience is that, for some people, the experience itself puts the Life Value top of mind. With due respect to Mr. Clausewitz, "natural" Ethical Warriors do not care about politics by other means. For them, the goals are simple: accomplish the mission, avoid unnecessary dying and killing, and hope to escape the psychological damage of the experience. For them, the priorities get straight rather quickly, and because they are focused on their roles as protectors, they retain their rational facilities despite the stress. However, for the poorly trained combatant under duress, the experience can be overwhelming and their actions more emotionally driven—and, as a result, unreliably effective and/or unreliably moral.

In MCMAP we set out to find a way to help people remain connected to the Life Value under adversity. We developed the Ethical Warrior concept as a way to provide participants with a certain level of clarity, comfort and sense of serenity as they navigate through the moral gray areas associated with the "fog of war." The job some warriors are called upon to perform—killing other human beings—is so abhorrent and unnatural to the vast majority of us that we need significant ethical training and preparation for that possibility beforehand. We also need help to recover from the experience of violence and death afterward. An approach to training Ethical Warriors must be consistent with the reality of how we holistically (physically, emotionally, intellectually, morally) experience, and attempt to cope with, traumatic situations like combat. There may be some who are "natural warriors" who can manage the horror of combat and killing without any special training, but they appear to be a very small percentage of the population. For others who are called to duty, a physical-mental-moral regimen can inoculate us from succumbing psychologically to the horrors of war. As unnatural as it appears to be for humans—even Marines—to take lives, behavior that protects life is very natural and cherished. Therefore, we say that an Ethical Warrior is a protector of life, killing only when necessary to protect the lives of self and others.

However, if the Life Value is not clarified, activated and reinforced beforehand, what we do when it is time for us to act—particularly under stress—may not be predictable. A lack of values lucidity may result in regretful incidents and, in war, atrocities. Philosophical confusion may even cause a deadly "freeze" at a critical time. In order to attain mental clarity and encourage ethical behavior under the stress of combat, we seek to develop a "Protector Mindset." The term Protector Mindset (sometimes referred to more generically as a "Combat Mindset") can be described as the ability to "do the right thing" under extreme emotional, psychological and physical adversity or stress. This includes the ability to override the emotions (including the fight, freeze or flight mechanism, if inappropriate for the situation) and act rationally to accomplish the mission in accordance with one's moral and physical training.

You may notice that there are several important concepts above highlighted in quotes—that is because they are difficult to pin down. If you haven't clarified your personal philosophy, you may not know what you will do when you need to act—particularly in combat—but also under duress of any kind. Philosophical confusion may even cause you to freeze and do nothing at a critical time.

According to hoplologist[46] Hunter Armstrong, the two basic forms of human combative behavior are predatory and affective. Predatory, or "effective" combative behavior, is that combative/aggressive behavior rooted in our evolution as a hunting mammal. "Affective" combative behavior is that aggressive/combative behavior rooted in our evolution as a group-social animal. When subjected to stress and danger some people behave "affectively," that is, emotionally. Emotional behavior is often ineffective in times of great danger when critical decisions need to be made and acted upon. We may "freeze" and fail to defend ourselves, or conversely, act in a wildly aggressive—and inappropriate— manner. As we discussed earlier, both behaviors can be exhibited by STRIKE "first-timers." As stressful as STRIKE can be, it is much less stressful than combat.

"Effective" behavior, on the other hand, is the behavior of a predator. The predator is cold and rational—like an animal intent on killing for food.

---

[46] Hoplology is the study of the evolution and development of human combative behavior. The International Hoplology website is http://www.hoplology.com.

Marine training—especially MCMAP training—is designed to develop an Ethical Marine Warrior, a "professional" protector of life. It is predator-*like*, in that it is efficient and professional. But the objective of a Protector Mindset is to have the mental perspective of a protector of life, killing humanely and respectfully, and only when necessary.

The Combat Mindset is sometimes referred to as *mushin* in Japanese. *Mushin* is often translated as "empty mind," but I think of it more as a "clear mind." It is important to realize that the Protector Mindset is not "empty," and that we don't suddenly have no emotions. The emotions are there, even the unhelpful ones, but our ethical and physical training allows us to "see through the spaces" between the emotions. In Japanese the word for "tactical space" is *kukan*. *Kukan* usually refers to the feeling of the space between the warrior and the opponent. I would propose that there is also a *kukan* within the mind of the warrior that exists "between" the emotions. I believe it is vital for the warrior to be able to manage and use both the external and internal *kukan*.

One of the components of certain types of combat training is an implicit or explicit encouragement to dehumanize the enemy. It might be conjectured that dehumanization, or objectivization, of the enemy makes it easier to overcome our natural revulsion to killing and make it easier to dispatch an opponent. I believe my own Marine training made me so coldly aggressive that I could not easily "turn it off," sometimes even with family and friends. Bob

Humphrey did not tell me that my attitude was wrong, per se, but only that there was a "better way." That way was the way of the Ethical Warrior. The mindset is totally different than what I thought it was based upon my training.

The Protector Mindset is comprised of three synergistic elements qualified by the Dual Life Value:

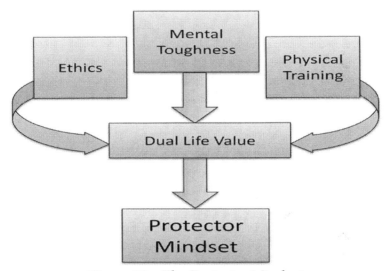

Figure 12 – The Protector Mindset

A combination of clarified ethics, effective warrior training and mental toughness (gained through practicing under adverse conditions) tends to allow us to overcome ineffective behavior under stress. Counterproductive, emotion-based thoughts and actions are "trumped" by the moral-physical drilled responses. We see through the "spaces" and do what needs to be done.

We are extremely hopeful that this ethics-based methodology will be effective in helping our warriors "do the right thing"—ethically, tactically and technically—in combat. We also believe it is proving itself to be useful in building resiliency. Our perspective is that the Ethical Warrior training can address the dangers of combat stress (Post Traumatic Stress Disorder, or PTSD), as well as the physical and psychological challenges faced by our wounded warriors.

In other words, our experience is proving that Ethical Warrior training delivered by MCMAP is a training regimen that can inoculate Marines from the stress of combat and mitigate the effects of PTSD. There is sufficient evidence that war and killing is so abhorrent to normal humans that it is inherently damaging to virtually everyone who participates. In fact, it could be said that it would be unnatural if people—even Marines—didn't get some degree of PTSD from exposure to war.

By the way, it is not just Marines or soldiers who get PTSD. Anyone subjected to extreme or prolonged stress and have it, too. The Ethical Warrior approach to dealing with stress can work for all of us in our daily lives.

From the perspective of the Life Value we see that there may be at least two forms of PTSD. As the Dual Life Value view of human nature describes the regard for self and others (sometimes self vs. others) as a delicate balance, we can see how the additional stresses of war and other traumatic events could make that balancing act particularly difficult. We might even temporarily (or permanently) find the scale tipped to the spilling point.

In some cases the balanced regard for self and others gets knocked off kilter toward the self (Figure 13).

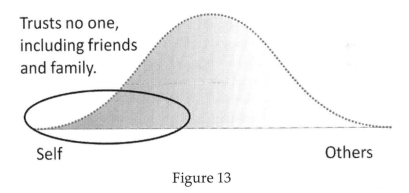

Trusts no one, including friends and family.

Self   Others

Figure 13

Exposure to extreme danger and stress makes the sufferer act overly suspicious of others or "paranoid," even after he or she leaves the war zone, even back at home. *Everybody* seems like the enemy, including friends and family. The others-protecting side of their human nature has been totally obscured by their pathology. We hear of severe PTSD cases of returning combatants who trust no one, to the point that they will even attack or kill their relatives, spouses and children. The sufferer is alienated from others and hyper-focused on his own survival. His or her "selfishness," however, brings no inner peace or happiness. Once a person gets this far off balance, as in any severe loss of stability, regaining a healthy equilibrium is very difficult.

Another form of PTSD manifests itself as feeling of self *worthlessness* (Figure 14).

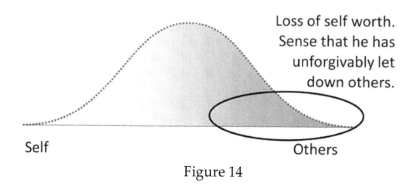

Loss of self worth. Sense that he has unforgivably let down others.

Self   Others

Figure 14

People with this form of PTSD feel that they should have done more to save their comrades; or they are filled with loathing for themselves for actions they took, or failed to take—or feel profound remorse for the people they killed. If they have dehumanized the enemy, that is also a factor.

From the perspective of the Ethical Warrior, the problem—whether the person is off kilter to the "self" side or the "other" side—is the same. He or she no longer considers him or herself a protector of self and all others. MCMAP re-activates that protector proclivity and guides the sufferer back into becoming that Ethical Protector again. One aspect of the training that we stress is others-protecting scenarios where the situation is such that the trainee must protect another against a third-party attacker (more about that later).

It bears repeating that research has shown that disrespect or dehumanization of the enemy (or, in the case of law enforcement officers, the criminal) exacerbates combat stress and "burn-out." MCMAP's Ethical Warrior training "calibrates the moral compass" by clarifying life as an inalienable right, a universal value shared by all people and, therefore, reaffirming the fact that "all men are created equal." Adherence to the Life Value philosophy safeguards our humanity—and sets us apart from immoral enemies (and criminals) who do not respect the lives of others outside of their "in-group." Adherence to the Ethical Warrior self image does two things: (1) it protects the warrior spiritually and psychologically, and (2) it gives him or her the philosophical "moral high ground" when in conflict.

Marines are taught to respect the enemies' lives, yet, to recognize—with guidance from the specific Rules of Engagement—when the enemies' behavior is life-threatening to fellow Marines and/or other people within their area of responsibility. In other words, Marines kill to protect life. This is most clear when you observe the difference in how respective enemy wounded are treated. If our enemies come upon one of our wounded and vulnerable soldiers, they will almost invariably "finish them off." When our enemies are wounded and no longer a threat, we render medical care.

As we have said, the Life Value is the "magnetic north" of the moral compass. The Ethical Warrior orients himself when under the stress of combat by using the Life Value as the supporting premise of his other moral values—including his USMC core values.

As discussed in the previous chapter, there is ample scientific evidence to support the premise that exercise cues the building blocks of the brain[47] and that intellectual lessons are retained more effectively when taught in conjunction with physical exercise. One of the anecdotal, yet most important and unheralded, phenomenon regarding the MCMAP and Ethical Protector training is that moral lessons, also, appear to be best delivered in the context of physical training. In other words, to develop Ethical Warriors, realistic physical training and values-based stories with emotional impact work best in combination, rather than separately.

In order to counteract the effects of PTSD, research has shown that a "purification process" is required after the stressful event(s). The purification process mediates the stress and grief of combat. MCMAP allows Marines to:

1. Decompress with challenging physical training, exercise and shared adversity in a controlled setting.

---

[47] Ratey M.D, John J., Spark: The Revolutionary New Science of Exercise and the Brain, 2008, p. 4

2. Share experiences with fellow Marines who have "been there," during guided discussions.
3. Recalibrate the moral compasses through the values-based stories.
4. Train and recover with other Marines.

MCMAP training develops Ethical Marine Warriors, provides a physical outlet for stress, and activates respect for all life (including that of the enemy). Most importantly, it functions as a post-combat "rite of purification" which is shared with fellow warriors.

Regardless of whether the PTSD sufferer's psychological imbalance is toward self or others—or oscillates back and forth—we can see that the root problem is similar in all cases. The person is no longer an "others-protector." It may be because he or she has lost empathy for others, or lost confidence in his or her own efficacy as a protector. Either way—or both—we focus on getting them back into the martial arts. We want to make them feel like protectors again. This, we feel, is a vital and underutilized tool for building or re-building resiliency to combat stress.

The feeling of inadequacy as a protector of others can understandably be even more acute for someone who has lost a limb or body function.

The fact is, however, that amputees can learn martial arts and can regain a level of physical efficacy as protectors. The following is a direct quote from a Marine Wounded Warrior amputee who practiced MCMAP as part of his recovery:

"The [physical, mental, character] synergy of MCMAP was a huge help to my recovery and rehabilitation. My big problem of transitioning back into the real world has been the idea that I killed and did something against God. The morals of MCMAP let me know that I was doing the right thing on both of my deployments and that I had just cause for my actions. Mind you I was on two heavy combat deployments but regardless the three disciplines [physical, mental, character] have helped tremendously. This is the one area where I would stress getting this information out to the wounded population in heavy doses. It helps.......end of sentence!

[MCMAP] is bottom line the most fulfilling, ethical and helpful program the US Marine Corps has in existence. I could not suggest a better situation to put Marines, injured or not, through. This program has helped me and I'm positive it would do the same for others."

If the moral-physical regimen can work for profoundly injured and stressed Marines, imagine what it could do for the rest of us. Obviously people can become stressed, at times profoundly so, by life's difficulties. You do not have to be a Marine to get PTSD; any traumatic event that threatens your safety or makes you feel out of control can cause PTSD.

Traumatic events besides war that can lead to PTSD include natural disasters, car or plane crashes, terrorist attacks, the sudden death of a loved one, rape, kidnapping, assault, sexual or physical abuse, and childhood neglect. According to the health organization Helpguide[48], PTSD can affect those who personally experience the catastrophe, those who witness it, and those who pick up the pieces afterwards, including emergency workers and law enforcement officers. Even people who *did not* physically experience the physical-trauma event (friends and/or family of the PTSD victim) can develop symptoms of PTSD. I strongly believe improper military and law enforcement training (especially demonization and dehumanization of the enemy) can also cause PTSD-like stress and the associated symptoms. PTSD also manifests itself differently from person to person. While the symptoms of PTSD most commonly develop in the hours or days following the traumatic event, it can sometimes take weeks, months, and even years before they appear.

A moral-physical program can be effective in ameliorating the impact of these tragic occurrences. Moral lessons appear to be best delivered in the context of physical training. If it works for Marines, why wouldn't it work for others? The exact details of the program for each kind of trauma must be appropriately customized to a certain extent, of course. It would have to make sense for each of us individually; and we are all effected differently. But because we all have the Life Value, anyone suffering

---

[48] Please see more at http://helpguide.org

from PTSD will likely benefit from the physical-moral regimen. It is certainly an approach worth trying, both inside and outside of the military and law enforcement arenas.

Why is martial arts practice so effective in both building Ethical Warriors and helping people overcome stress? The book "Sparks" provides insight into the physiological benefits of exercise, but the simple answer to why moral lessons and exercise go together is: that they just do. Perhaps we will have a scientific answer sometime in the future. In the meantime, why don't more people practice martial arts for the obvious benefits? Many people I speak with feel they are "too old," "too out of shape," "nursing an old injury," or quite frankly, "too important to get hurt." If you believe that about yourself, I say, "So...participate at a level that makes sense for you. But participate." For one thing, you will be leading by example, and that is important. We all lead or set an example for someone. The other reason is that *we* need it. Regardless of our experience or maturity level, a physical-mental-moral regimen is necessary and ethically reinforcing for all of us. *Unselfish* protector training contributes to the *others* side of the Life Value. The others side of the Life Value calls for responsible self-development in order to contribute to the group. Besides, we all could use confidence and skills.

As we get older we can become good at rationalizing away insecurity and inefficacy, but this is self-delusion. We are never too old to benefit from moral activation and physical exercise; and ethics are moral-physical. Not everyone needs martial arts training to be ethical, of course—some people just "have it." But others need an activating routine. In my experience it is harder to make a moral person physical than to make a physical person ethical. Can you see that when you cease becoming physical, you risk becoming less confident in your moral actions? Simple exercise in the gym or jogging around the park just can't activate the others-protecting proclivity like martial arts training can.

I have focused on warriors in this section, but I believe that Ethical Warriors set an example for all of us. There have been many great warriors over the course of history—people who have defended others, often at great risk to themselves. One thing that is consistent with the great majority of them is that they did not think of themselves as heroes. In fact, they were pretty much just like you and me. They recognized the need to accept the responsibility of protecting their families, communities and/or country as "only natural." Some of them were also called upon to defend people who were not of their own country. Some of them were even called upon to protect their enemies, but that's what warriors do: They protect and defend.

Some people think that being a warrior is about killing. This is misguided. Anyone can kill. A homicidal maniac kills people, yet he or she is certainly not a warrior. Yes, warriors do sometimes kill, but their motivations are very specific; they kill only as defenders and protectors. This is not an easy concept, and at first may even sound like a contradiction in terms—kill to protect life? That certainly seems like a paradox. So, we will continue to explore this idea in more depth. At the end, you decide which is more consistent with your ideal of a warrior: a killer or a protector?

In the meantime, we might ask: is killing a natural part of life? If so, how is it natural? We have been saying that killing is *not* natural; protecting life is natural. But, let us consider a bigger picture. What did you eat today? An animal or plant was killed to make that meal. Obviously, big fish eat little fish, lions eat gazelles, etc. So we are forced to acknowledge that killing is part of the circle of life. But killing for what purpose? In these cases, it is killing in order to eat, which is necessary to life—in other words, killing to protect life. We humans acknowledge that fact in subtle ways. In most cultures of the world there is a prayer before meals to give thanks. Thanks to whom? Some people would say God, because God, in His bounty, has made the food available. Other cultures, particularly aboriginal or animist cultures, offer up a prayer to the spirit of the animal or plant itself as a natural gesture of respect and acknowledgement that a life was sacrificed so that others might live. I don't know what happened in your home growing up, but I was sometimes told by my grandmother that if I didn't finish everything on my plate that it was a...*sin!* Why? Because the food would have been wasted; this meant that a life would have been wasted.

These are pretty clear and straightforward examples. When it comes to killing for reasons other than direct subsistence, it gets trickier. Is it ethical, for instance, to kill in self defense? Why would someone try to kill you? What do people kill over? Usually they kill over relative values, such as behavior, race, or ethnicity. People also kill for control of your money or property. Or just because they like the feeling of power over others. Superseding the Life Value with a relative value, as we have discussed, is morally wrong. It is ethically justified to kill when necessary to protect life. But *only* to protect life.

There are some pacifist groups, Mennonites and some Buddhists, for example, who eschew all violence. Humphrey told me of a conversation he had with a pacifist who said he would never use violence, even against someone who was trying to kill him (hopefully he will never have to back up that claim). But when Professor Humphrey asked him whether he would defend his child, the man quickly said, "Yes, of course, that's only natural." The Dual Life Value operates again.

There are also many misconceptions about the essence of the martial arts themselves. Many people think of martial arts in terms of winning a fight. Certainly there is that aspect in sport fighting, but there is a clear difference between martial arts as a sport, and the art of warriorship. When people fight for sport, they fight for themselves—perhaps to exercise their natural competitive urges or to win a trophy. There is really nothing wrong with sport fighting. Both my sons wrestled competitively and I was all for it. My own nose has a bend in it that I wasn't born with. So I am not against martial sports, as long as they don't get too violent or make the participants too selfish.

Many people also think of martial arts in terms of "self-defense." Certainly, self defense is ethical and martial art skills can be used to protect the self. Yet, *anyone* would protect themselves if they could. That does not necessarily make them a warrior—or ethical, for that matter. Homicidal maniacs will defend themselves. You do not have to be a warrior to defend yourself—or want to. For now, we can certainly say that Ethical Warriorship is not just about self-defense. Warriors don't fight only for themselves; they fight for their countries, and communities, their families and friends—they fight for *others*. Warriorship is about defending others at the risk of your own safety—perhaps your own life. This is a profound and fundamental philosophical difference from the typical purpose of a sport fight. Therefore, the notion of "winning" needs to be re-examined when it comes to the Ethical Warrior. War is not a sport. Historians may see wars in terms of winners and losers, but the ones who fight the wars know that it is not quite so clear-cut: accomplish the mission, avoid unnecessary dying and killing, and deal with the physical and psychological aftermath. That is war.

Are our citizen protectors—such as paramedics, firefighters, emergency room doctors and nurses, etc.—warriors? They certainly are heroes, but I would say that there is one difference: although they may risk their own lives to save those of others, rarely are they required to *kill* to protect life[49]. That, to me, is a profound distinction.

The training philosophy and methodology for training as an Ethical Warrior is also different than that for sport training. I remember one of the first times that I stayed in Japan for a prolonged period. I was living in Noda at the inn described earlier. Besides being a little homesick, I also eventually got a terrific cold. Hatsumi Sensei saw that I was suffering and invited me back to his house. "I am a doctor," he said. Well, I knew he was a bone doctor, I didn't think he was an internist; but, of course, I went.

His old house was drafty and smelly. He had no children, but he had three dogs, forty (yes forty) cats, an owl, a turkey, many fish and a bunch of turtles. We went into the unbelievably cluttered sitting room and he told me to sit down. He then rummaged around in a chipped white cabinet until he came out with this huge jar filled with a milky clearish liquid. At the bottom of the jar was a dead snake. Now, I

---

[49] Warriors also realize that in war innocents are at risk of be killed in connection with their actions. That is an added burden.

recognized that snake. Having trained in jungle warfare in the Northern Training Area on the island of Okinawa, I knew that snake to be a *habu*. We hated them because they hunted at night, located and attacked their prey by honing in on body heat, and were quite poisonous. Nobody was keen to practice night ambushes lying around in the jungle with *habus* possibly in the area. To say the least, I was a little dubious when Hatsumi Sensei poured a big serving of the snake-marinating liquid (which, by the way, was *shochu*, a kind of raw rice vodka) into a dirty tea cup, handed it to me and said "drink, drink." I looked at it, scales floating on top, held my breath, closed my eyes and choked it down. Sensei quickly poured another and again said "drink, drink." So I drank, drank.

Funny, in a couple of minutes I started feeling better—or perhaps stopped feeling bad. Actually, I felt a little like I had entered a dream world. The lights were low, the wind was rattling the windows, we were huddled around a small gas heater for warmth, and I was sitting alone with the grandmaster of a 900 year old secret martial art tradition.

Then Sensei did a very unusual thing. He said I could ask him anything I wanted. Often, Japanese martial arts teachers don't allow questions. If you are lucky enough to be accepted into the training, you shut your mouth and do whatever the teacher tells you to do. This may go on for years until you finally understand the lessons on your own by osmosis—or quit.

So on this mysterious-feeling night with a head slightly swimming from sickness and the snake wine, I tried to think of a question. What would you have asked? It was an opportunity of a lifetime. Here is what I asked: "How did your teacher, Takamatsu Sensei, teach you 900 years of martial arts in 15 years?" Some question, if I may say so myself. And Sensei had some answer. He said, "I can teach you in 10! But...you have to listen to me, and train the way *I* tell you to train, not the way *you* think you should train."

I guess the inference was that if I tried to figure out the secret of true warriorship on my own it might take me...900 years. But the important point, I think, is that people have studied the art of war and the art of protecting life for hundreds of years. And there are secrets, and there are things that work better than others. But it is a difficult and sometimes counter-intuitive process to learn these secrets. It is easy to go the wrong way; we are dealing with human conflict, violence and killing, after all. I am still trying to absorb it all, even after 30 plus years of training, but there are shortcuts. You don't need 900 years, but you have to do it right. Some of the core principles are very counter-intuitive. Respect for your enemy is one of them. It may be very surprising to some people, for example, to consider that warriors, first and foremost, must be ethical.

The same is true of the Life Value concept and methodology for resolving conflict. It is not a secret...yet, it is. Most everyone has the potential to access this truest and most fundamental value, but not everyone does. It takes clarity, it takes activation, and it takes practice. Perhaps sacrifice. Sound familiar? It is the same basic process that we use to create Ethical Warriors.

The first rule is that Ethical Warriors are "protectors," rather than killers. It makes a lot of sense when you think about it. We know, for example, that young, patriotic men and women join the Marines and the other services or the law enforcement agencies, to defend their country and protect their communities—not to become killers. Ethical Warrior training is designed to enhance that natural protector proclivity.

So, here is a hypothetical question for you (actually, it is a real question that was posed to me by combat correspondent and Pulitzer Prize nominee Robert Drury in a bar during an interview): "You are a 19-year-old Marine lance corporal and you've just returned from a foot patrol in the Western Cluster in Helmand Province—the Western Cluster's Motto: Where Foreigners Come To Die. Sure enough, during that patrol your best buddy steps on an IED (Improvised Explosive Device) that kills him instantly and blows off the legs of another friend. Does the code of the Ethical Warriorship really apply to the guy that planted that bomb?" In other words, should we summarily kill, or try to avoid killing, immoral enemy combatants?

I shared this question with Bob Humphrey's son, Galen, in private correspondence. I will let him answer:

> "I just caught the guy who set the IED (improvised explosive device) in the road that killed my buddy. If I turn him over to intelligence is there *any* possibility the prisoner could provide information regarding other IED locations or information about others supporting his cause, and/or how he was recruited? If any info garnered from the prisoner might save the life of another person—innocent road walker, or combat personnel—doesn't that smack of the need (ethical imperative), for a humane approach when dealing with such deadly enemy combatants? I allow him to live in order to save lives.
>
> The conflict is bigger than I, the individual. Ethical Warriors are necessary to win the bigger conflict. The challenge with Ethical Warriorship is: one has to be rational, i.e. very well trained. Easily said, but difficult in the emotional fields of war. *War*: meaning when people are dying miserably, sometimes in your arms. To maintain rationality *and* a sense of morality under such awful duress is heroic.
>
> Our men and women are trained as 'protector/defenders of life.' They kill, when necessary, in the name of protecting/defending life. Our men and women must learn why it is necessary to allow a subdued combatant to live;

that monster-like being might help in the mission to protect/defend others. You rein in the limbic system *in order to protect life.* The emotional killing of a prisoner of war can lead to *more* deaths; not only is it considered murder, it's stupid in that it can get more friends (or you) killed later. It might feel good for the moment, but it ain't very smart or rational—nor is it *ethical because the selfish action has just jeopardized the lives of others."*

People ask (and this is a big one): If the training is ethics-based, wouldn't that tend to make the participants "soft," or "too nice?" This is a question we agonized over when developing MCMAP. It comes down to this: should Marines be trained as killers or protectors? Are "protectors" as prepared for the realities of war as "killers?" Will ethics training somehow make them "soft" and less capable of accomplishing the mission—maybe get themselves and others killed? Will they be looking down the barrel of their rifles at an enemy who is trying to kill them and hear in their minds, "his life and the life of his loved ones are as important to him as mine are to me?" Will the Ethical Warrior then hesitate to pull the trigger? All valid questions. But hesitation does not seem to be the case based upon my research. If a combatant doesn't pull the trigger, it is not because he is having a conflict of values; rather, it is probably because he is in shock and not properly trained for, or inoculated to, the shocking realities of violence. Our greatest combat heroes of the two World Wars were

Sgt. Alvin York and Audie Murphy, who both won the Medal of Honor for valor while killing many enemy soldiers. Were they considered mean, or were they known to be "nice boys" whose heroics were surprises in combat? Definitely the latter.

Doubt on whether emphasizing the "protector approach" makes Ethical Warriors soft still exists and much more research is needed and underway. Anecdotally, one may hear both sides of the argument from sincere people who have "been there." I have read many well-meaning books and watched many videos on "street survival" and how to prepare for the realities of unexpected violence. There are good points and ideas in many of them. The tone of these books and videos, however, worries me. They typically represent an "out thug the thug" approach that can be tactically sensible, but psychologically damaging. This kind of training can actually *give* the participant PTSD.

After a lot of thought, I still don't definitively know whether the protector approach is the most tactical, but my research leads me to believe that it is. Consider the following scenarios: (1) You are walking through a forest and you see a killer grizzly bear; would you be afraid? Almost definitely so. (2) You are walking through a forest and see a grizzly bear with two cubs, would you be less afraid—or more? Most people would say "more afraid." Why? Because, even in nature, it seems the protector is more dangerous than the killer. All things being equal, protectors are more dangerous than killers—and to anyone who threatens them and the people they are sworn to protect.

One thing we do know is there are severe psychological risks associated with training moral people to become killers. As we have mentioned, human beings are not natural-born killers. Historically the military often has used operant conditioning techniques to help combatants overcome autonomic tendencies that are ineffective or inefficient in combat. Counter-productive tendencies, such as freezing, fleeing, fighting with "hot blood" rather than cool professionalism, etc., are controllable by training, but also benefit from grounding in the Life Value.

A combination of ethical clarification, mental toughness and appropriate physical training can help us overcome ineffective emotional and autonomic proclivities and keep us effectively safe without fostering a psychologically unhealthy mindset. Two pieces are key—ethics and training. Otherwise, we risk using the more "intuitive," but philosophically incorrect (and psychologically dangerous) technique of dehumanization and demonization of the enemy, to make the killing "easier." We already know that dehumanization exacerbates PTSD. You may be able to temporarily trick the brain into thinking that your enemy isn't really human, but you can't supersede the Life Value—not without risking severe negative psychological repercussions.

Another important consideration is that being an Ethical Warrior can be more physically dangerous. A tremendous amount of training is necessary for most of us to be effective protectors. You can't just read this—or any—book. You have to train in the physical skills of the warrior. I often encounter people who want to discuss (or debate) the philosophical aspects of the Life Value. In other words, they want to discuss their relative viewpoints without considering the fact that life and death underpins everything we do. I listen, but won't enter into that kind of dialogue unless the person will acknowledge that Life is a objective value and that it applies to self and all others. Without that premise, discussion is pointless. In the ivory tower world of ethical relativism, eventually, all perspectives are defensible. That is why, I believe, Humphrey was only able to glimpse the essence of the Dual Life Value because of his experiences on Iwo Jima. Yes, he *observed* this subtle, yet core, aspect of human nature. He did not intuit it.

I have often asked myself why Humphrey was able to see the Life Value and articulate it while so many other philosophers came close but did not see it as completely or in the same way. I have made myself into an amateur academic by reading many works of the great philosophers and thinkers, but they all fall short, in my opinion, of the symmetry, logic and simple elegance of the Dual Life Value concept.

For example, there is a school of philosophy called Empiricism. Empiricism asserts that knowledge comes *entirely* from experience, as opposed to pure thinking or intuition. Empiricism, in a nutshell, says that information compiled by observation speaks for itself. Observation was Humphrey's method, right? So how did Humphrey arrive at the Dual Life Value as a universal, intrinsic value while the Empiricists suggest a "blank slate" view of human nature? Here is a possible reason: remember the story of the Marine sergeant on Iwo Jima who refused to volunteer when the platoon was safe and in a protected area? Empiricists who would have observed that incident might have come to the conclusion that self preservation is the first law of nature. And they would have gotten it all wrong. As you recall, the next day when lives were on the line, the sergeant did the exact opposite—insisting that he be the one to take on the almost sure suicide mission. Unless the Empiricists had also been there that next day (unlikely), the initial conclusions they might have drawn would be flawed due to incomplete observation, resulting in inaccurate data, leading to a faulty conclusion. Totally understandable—after all, how many of us have ever experienced an Iwo Jima situation when all of our relative values are stripped away, leaving only the Dual Life Value?

The Empiricists were right about one thing, however; life is not a purely intellectual exercise. War certainly isn't—at least for the combatants in the thick of it. I sincerely hope that you, the reader, never have to kill anyone. But, you might have to in order to defend yourself and others. And you probably would do it if it were absolutely necessary, because it is in your nature to be a protector. And it would be ethical.

Let's explore briefly the fact that the nuances of the Life Value, as described by Humphrey, are not covered in the countless books on philosophy. I believe that one of the reasons, as in the case of Newton and the apple, is that it was just not observed by the right person at the right time with the right eye for it. Without his experiences on Iwo Jima it is almost inconceivable that Humphrey would have grasped the elusive essence of the Dual Life Value. As Frans De Waal says in his book, "The Age of Empathy," the most "striking examples of empathetic perspective-taking, both in humans and animals, concern single incidents." It is difficult or impossible to set up a laboratory experiment that mimics the complex workings of human nature under real life and death circumstances, for obvious reasons. Dr. DeWaal relates an incident that he personally observed at a pond in Balboa Park in San Diego. The Park was full of people when a small child raced through the crowd, jumped into the pond and quickly sank. It happened so quickly that everyone was frozen. The child's mother suddenly appeared, looked quickly around, guessed what had happened, and jumped right into the pond—without hesitation and fully dressed. She popped up a moment later with the toddler in her arms. If she had not acted so decisively, it is anyone's guess how long it might have taken to find the child in the murky water.

Here we see alertness to another's situation at a level that's impossible to mimic in a lab. We can ask people what they would do under circumstances, and we can test them under mildly upsetting conditions, but no one is going to reenact the near drowning of a child to see how its parents react. Yet this sort of situation, which is essentially untestable, produces by far the most interesting altruism and the actions most relevant to survival.[50]

If you are inclined to believe that this behavior only applies to a mother for her child, remember the line of firefighters walking up the stairs of the World Trade Center on September 11, 2001 to save countless people they had never met and did not know. Everybody else was running down.

Consider, also, the story of Wesley Autrey, a 50-year-old construction worker and Navy veteran who was waiting for a New York City subway on January 3, 2007 with his two daughters, Syshe, 4, and Shuqui, 6.

Nearby, a man collapsed, his body convulsing. Mr. Autrey and two women rushed to help.... The man, Cameron Hollopeter, 20, managed to get up, but then stumbled to the platform edge and fell to the tracks, between the two rails. The headlights of the No. 1 train appeared. "I had to make a split decision," Mr. Autrey said.

So he made one, and leapt.

---

[50] De Waal, Frans. The Age of Empathy. 2009. pp. 103.

Mr. Autrey lay on Mr. Hollopeter, his heart pounding, pressing him down in a space roughly a foot deep. The train's brakes screeched, but it could not stop in time. Five cars rolled overhead before the train stopped, the cars passing inches from his head, smudging his blue knit cap with grease. Mr. Autrey heard onlookers' screams. "We're O.K. down here," he yelled, "but I've got two daughters up there. Let them know their father's O.K." He heard cries of wonder, and applause.

Mr. Autrey refused medical help, because, he said, nothing was wrong. He did visit Mr. Hollopeter in the hospital before heading to his night shift. "I don't feel like I did something spectacular; I just saw someone who needed help," Mr. Autrey said. "I did what I *felt* was right [Emphasis added]."[51]

The willingness of human beings to risk and, perhaps, sacrifice their lives for others seems to reflect a deep and intrinsic self-giving/species-preserving proclivity—at least in some of us. It may be innate to a certain extent, but whatever the root, life-saving and others-protecting acts give the person that performs them incomparable feelings of serenity and nobility.

To be fair, Francis Bacon did seem to have a feel for the concept of an inherent self and others-

---

[51] "Man Is Rescued by Stranger on Subway Tracks," by Cara Buckley, New York Times, January 3, 2007

balanced moral sense. He is quoted in Will Durant's "The Pleasures of Philosophy:"[52] "A remarkable sentence in *The Advancement of Learning* contains in outline an entire theory of secular ethics. 'All things,' says the great Chancellor, 'are endued with an appetite to two kinds of good; the one, as the thing is a whole in itself' [self good], 'the other as it part of some greater whole' [communal good]; 'and this latter is more worthy and more powerful than the other, as it tends to the conservation of a more ample form.' That is to say, morality, like immorality, has its basis in human nature..."

Bacon obviously had a glimpse of the Life Value. Humphrey went a lot further and also identified the physical-moral connection. That is where the martial arts part of the story becomes integral.

It is interesting that most people I meet would love to have self and others protection skills. Yet, they don't pursue them. They say they are too old, or too busy, or too important, or they have a knee problem or other previous injury, or they are too lazy—or they just don't want to think about it. To consider the realities of being hurt or killed is just too negative for some people. So they don't. The problem with that, of course, is that if you live your life with blinders regarding the Life Value, you tend to focus on the other values—the relative ones. Soon, it is easy to become unbalanced and unhappy.

---

[52] W. Durant. The Pleasures of Philosophy. Touchstone. Pp 90.

This book was originally envisioned as a companion to the actual combatives and conflict resolution courses that others and I provide the Marines and law enforcement officers. One of the reactions I have had from some people who have read drafts of this book is that "there are some interesting stories, but isn't the Dual Life Value essentially just a variation on the Golden Rule?" I had hoped that I would be able to articulate my belief that the Dual Life Value is even more "essential" and nuanced than our usual and common understanding of the Golden Rule. I may or may not have accomplished that goal.

However, the criticism is correct in one very important aspect—there *is* something missing. It is the actual martial arts training itself. In other words, the Dual Life Value isn't best taught intellectually or through the stories. It is best when it is *experienced and practiced*. That experience can be contextual, but it can also be carefully created in a synergistic—intellectual, emotional, physical—training regimen like MCMAP or other Ethical Protector training courses that include the physical skills.

Yet, even if you never do train, the Life Value—and the **"physical + moral = ethical"** concept—applies to everybody. So I offer this book to anyone who might be interested in the Dual Life Value philosophy from an intellectual perspective, or the stories from an emotional standpoint; and, perhaps, some people will also be inspired to start training.

It is also the case that there are those who possess the heart of an Ethical Warrior but are not "on the job" as law enforcement officers or military personnel, or they may not have the physical capability to practice martial arts. I encourage everyone to stay physical. Somehow. Physical confidence helps moral people act—do *something* to help, and not freeze in time of need—even if it is "only" to call 911 or yell for help. Those, too, are potentially lifesaving actions, aren't they?

Clarifying, activating and practicing the Life Value in your life works well in combination with outside reading and/or classroom instruction on related topics, values stories, etc. But, in my opinion, it works most reliably within the context of a regular martial arts regimen—even if you never do end up having to protect yourself or a loved one. Ethical Warriorship is a physical-mental-moral lifestyle. If you are missing one of the legs, the stool won't stand as it could.

But, again, why martial arts? Ethics are ultimately physical-mental-moral. Moral people may want to step up and do the right thing, but they often lack the physical courage and skills. As stated before, martial arts give them the necessary skills and confidence— *even if they never have to use them!* You often hear that the most experienced martial arts masters never have to fight. Perhaps their experience allows them to sense conflict before it erupts and subtly impact the situation by words or actions so that the conflict never occurs; or maybe something about their very presence discourages unnecessary conflict. I believe that the physical skills and confidence can make a difference in averting or controlling conflict. And that is why Ethical Warrior training includes—and may require—martial arts, especially for those involved in professions like law enforcement and the military. But citizen warriors should consider training in the martial arts as well. It has become clear that the code of the Ethical Warrior could apply to almost anyone.

If you do decide to seek out training, I have one more piece of advice: Look carefully for the right teacher. You may be tempted to just go to the most convenient place down the street. Unfortunately, it may just not be that easy and convenient. In my case, I had to travel to Japan to find that right martial arts teacher.

Another saying is "when the student is ready, the teacher appears." That seems to be what happened to me when I met Masaaki Hatsumi, and also, Bob Humphrey. Meeting both of those men was pretty darn good luck: two great teachers in one lifetime! I hope you are half as lucky as I have been. On the other hand, I sometimes consider the fact that I was probably so off the ethical mark that I actually needed three fathers—my own father, Hatsumi *and* Humphrey—to help me find the path I am fortunate to be on now.

Undeniably, warriorship is a physical, as well as, a philosophical and spiritual path. That physical part is so important. I remember discussing with Humphrey the case of a man, as reported in the Washington, D.C. news, who stood and watched as his own wife was being beaten by a neighbor. Later, he explained to the police that he "did not want to get involved." No, I think he would have *loved* to have gotten involved; he was just too shocked, afraid, morally confused, and unskilled to act—even to protect his own wife. That couldn't have felt good.

These ethically challenging scenarios occur all the time. I recall taking my son to the batting cage one rainy day to hit some baseballs. It turned out that I was not the only one to have that bright idea: there was a long line of kids waiting at each of the two pitching machines. A minute of observation made it clear that, by unspoken agreement, each kid was putting in a token and hitting ten balls—and then going to the end of the line so others could get a fair turn. The process was working nicely until...one father grabbed his son who was leaving the cage after his ten balls. The father put another token in and pushed the kid back in for ten more swings. My kid wasn't even in line yet, so I watched to see what the other fathers would do. They did...nothing. Amazing. So, finally, I stepped up to the father who had forced his son to take an extra turn and said, "Sir, it looks like people have agreed to take one turn then go to the end of the line. May I ask why you took two turns?" He said, "This is taking too long, I am leaving my kid in there and you should, too." I said, "Well, I am not going to do that, and you are not going to do that again, either. Your son goes to the back of the line like everybody else." He grumbled something, but he sent his kid to the back of the line. I turned around to look for my son, and the father of one of the boys in line sidled up to me and said out of the corner of his mouth, "That guy is an @#*$%^&." I said, "No, you are, for not doing the right thing for your own son." There was very little risk that the situation would have escalated into a physical fight, yet this guy couldn't act, even on behalf of his own child. The foul-mouthed father may have been moral, but he didn't have the courage to be ethical. That couldn't have felt good, either.

Ethics are moral-physical, as we have highlighted in this book repeatedly. The concept of the Ethical Warrior represents the Life Value in its most elemental manifestation. The Ethical Warrior embraces the universal Life Value and Human Equality. Adherence to the Life Value and respect for *all* others is closer to our true human nature than a tribal (atavistic) perspective. But it often takes leadership to help us overcome the "us-them" mentality.

Moral people need leaders. Watch someone cut in front of ten people at the movie ticket line and no one says a thing…unless one person says, "Hey, get to the back of the line!" Then what happens? Right. More often than not, the other nine people start speaking up, "Yeah, you heard him." "Yeah, get to the back of the line." It would be nice if we had one Ethical Warrior in every movie line, on every school bus, in every restaurant, and in every bleacher section of every football game. If for no other reason than to provide a little leadership so that the other moral people could be inspired to be ethical, too!

Humphrey, in his work combating Ugly Americanism against allied peoples overseas, often said that the truly disrespectful few who tried to foment violence against the local inhabitants always thought they were expressing the will of most of the Americans. Tough talk by 10% to 20% of the Americans in a culture-shocked population always convinced many of the other 80% to 90% that everyone believed in violence. Whereas actually, according to his studies, less than 1% of the culture-shocked Americans were actually willing to use violence against the locals. The rest was just angry talk.

Again, Ethical Warriors are protectors rather than killers. The paradoxical-sounding statement "we kill to protect life" is the key. When a person kills to protect life, it can be difficult, but it is ethical. When one kills to further relative values (my tribe, my religion, my color, my country, my anger, my revenge, my fear, my greed) it is immoral. That unethical path will almost certainly cause *more* conflict—and damage one's own spirit.

However, it takes real character and self confidence to resist falling in with the rabble-rousing of the truly unethical few. Ethical Warriors must be persons of character. Character means living in accordance with your own, most noble, human nature—under stress. Character starts with the number one universal value: respect for life. As stated, all of the great moral values, including honor, courage and commitment (but also liberty, the pursuit of happiness, honesty, freedom, etc.), are only great and moral when tied to the Life Value.

The ability to live and perform one's duties in accordance with your values (and your training) requires a strong mind. When confronted with situations like war and criminal violence—or even an unethical person in a movie theater—a normal untrained response is shock, confusion, anger, fear, unreliable action and/or the inability to act.

A strong mind that is able to access the physical skills and ethics of the warrior can be called the "Protector Mindset" or the "Ethical Warrior Mindset." Because emotions are controllable, the Ethical Warrior Mindset allows the warrior to overcome the fear, stress and fog of combat, but also adversity in everyday life. This mindset allows warriors to function as reliable professionals—in accordance with their physical training and the universal values, rather than relative values and emotions such as fear, anger, shock and grief. Do warriors *feel* fear, anger, shock and grief? Absolutely. But that does not drive the Ethical Warrior's *actions;* their actions are driven by their training, which facilitates rationality and their adherence to the Life Value. Their relative values spring from the Life Value, making those values moral. The Ethical Warrior mindset is a result of effective physical training and a clarified value system. In the fog of war—on the battlefield or in the boardroom—we calibrate our moral compass using the Life Value as the true north. We see through the *spaces* between the emotions. Our decisions are based on the facts as we see them clearly, and underpinned by respect for the people whose lives are impacted by our decisions.

When the great warrior sages said that martial arts protect the spirit, *that* is what they were talking about: the ability to participate in the most horrifying thing a human can do, killing another human being, but do it in a way that is ethical—respectful of the life that must be taken, and also protective of their own warrior spirit.

I teach well over one hundred martial arts classes and seminars every year in my home town and around the world. I often find that people are just looking for something new—a new technique, a new "style," a new philosophy. Remember what we said about clarifying, activating and *sustaining* the Life Value? The longer I train, the clearer it becomes to me that the purpose of martial arts is not to learn the latest fancy punch, kick or throw, but to *practice*— practice being a protector, practice living the Life Value in thought, word and deed. Therefore, I think that once you embark on it, the Ethical Warrior training must be ongoing. The biggest challenge is that, without a sustainment regimen, the clarification and activation parts tend to "wear off" or become occluded by our relative values. We must sustain our warrior ethic by continuous practice. It is no surprise that many of us are admonished to go to church every

Sunday; look what many of us are doing by Saturday night! Observe, also, the sustainment methodology of the Muslim faith—pray five times a day. For those in the warrior professions, sustainment means at least a few hours a week of the physical training with the moral lessons incorporated into the lesson. Physical and moral training creates a strong, protector mindset.

Ethics, communication skills, physical skills— these, I believe, are the three essential elements of the Ethical Warrior's approach to conflict resolution. They sound like three distinct things, but they are all ingredients to a necessary whole. You can't have one without the others. Take water, hops, yeast and malt. Stir it together in a glass. What you get is...well, it's not beer. (You may have wondered how long it was going to take an Irish-American Marine to start talking about beer. If you are not a beer drinker, think of baking a cake—the analogy is the same.)

Creating Ethical Warriors is obviously not the same as brewing beer or baking a cake. But, though most military and law enforcement training regimens provide a fairly robust ethical, tactical and technical training curriculum—all the "ingredients" for an effective physical approach to conflict resolution—the parts don't always add up to an effective whole. The hope is that if you have all the right training ingredients then somehow these pieces will synergize within the person, making him or her into a motivated and skillful professional. Sometimes it happens, but it is still not easy to "brew" a great

Ethical Warrior. Experience has shown that superior results may require more than just the right elements—those elements have to be introduced into the training in a *synergistic* way. Most training focuses on each of these elements in isolation. One learns to shoot on the range, move tactically in a shoot-house, and communicate and act ethically in a classroom. The time devoted to each of these areas follows the same order. The most time is devoted to technical training, less to individual and group tactics, and even less still to ethics. This approach tends to reinforce a paradigm that resolves conflict by selecting a technique, adjusting the technique (perhaps, belatedly) based on the tactical considerations, and finally deciding whether the technique is legally permissible. That is backwards.

In 1985, an incident in a major Eastern city illustrates well the problem caused by disconnected ethics, tactics and techniques. The metropolitan police department was faced with one of the most dangerous situations in law enforcement. A group of armed and committed radical activists were refusing to vacate a fortified house. Weapons fire was being exchanged, and efforts to penetrate the barricaded structure with tear gas canisters were ineffective.

Faced with these critical circumstances, those in charge chose to employ a military technique in a law enforcement situation resulting in the most famous, and perhaps only, use of aerial bombardment in American law enforcement history. Four pounds of high explosives were dropped from a helicopter onto the roof of the house. The intention was to breach the barricaded roof in order to introduce tear gas into the building—the resulting fire from the bombs caused the death of eleven people and destroyed sixty-five homes.

The political, legal and personal ramifications of this action reverberated for years. For our purposes, the key point is that techniques and tactics were employed that were in direct conflict with the Life Value: protect your life and the life of others, all others, even the adversary if possible. The desire to break a dangerous stalemate caused leaders to choose an unproven technique with consequences that were not protective of life. The technique drove the tactics which led to the ethical failure.

An alternative model is to approach conflicts from the perspective of the Life Value, which leads to choosing appropriate tactics to ensure the protection of self and others, and finally to the employment of the most effective techniques. This model also requires a shift in training philosophy. To the greatest extent possible, the Life Value must be taught *as part of* tactical and technical training. This provides an integrated understanding of moral values in action, which is the definition of ethics.

So, how would the training look? MCMAP is designed as a synergistic program consisting of three main elements:

1. **Character** — Ethical Warrior Training

2. **Mental** — Military Skills and Mindset Training
3. **Physical** — Martial Combatives and Combat Conditioning

Notably, again, the character piece is considered to be the core of the Program.

But, in the same way you "brew" beer by using the activating principle of fermentation which creates something new (and delicious) from otherwise separate ingredients, you need activating principles to develop Ethical Warriors. First of all, we have learned that it is unproductive to teach ethics only in the classroom. The Marines—and everybody else—tend to fall asleep! We now know that the best way to integrate ethics into the training is right in the middle of the physical training (tactical and/or technical). Train for a bit, get the juices flowing, and then interject "values-tie-ins"—stories with a strong emotional impact that inspire moral behavior (e.g., The Hunting Story). In other words, do the ethical, tactical and technical training all together!

By now, it should not be a surprise that martial skills training is an activating ingredient. The reason is that physical exercise and shared adversity prepare the heart and mind for a deep understanding and acceptance of the Life Value. And, why waste time moving people to a classroom to talk about values? Hit them while they are open-minded and energized. It just works better. I said martial arts training, because that seems to work the best, but any physical activity that includes shared adversity sets the stage for values learning. Adventure-based team-building training, like ropes courses, may also create a good atmosphere for ethical clarification.

I slipped in a little phrase, above, that is often used when talking about enlightenment, especially in Eastern philosophies. It is *thought, word*[53] *and deed.* Other ways of saying it are "physical, mental, moral," or "mind, body, spirit," etc. Previously we defined ethics as morals plus physical action (Moral + Physical = Ethical). Another important piece is the "word." There is a Japanese warrior saying *bun bu ryu do* (literally "way of literary and military arts together") which means that a warrior must be as adept with the pen as he is with the sword. Ideally, samurai were expected to be gentlemen warriors — to be as learned in books as they were in the martial arts. Yet, without the Life Value of self and all others as the superseding perspective, how can we be sure that the lessons of scholarship will be used ethically? You would agree that there are many quite educated, yet very unethical, people in our world. In fact, I am very much more afraid of a highly educated, white-collar criminal than a less-educated street thug.

Another fact is that scholars often live sheltered from the realities faced by the many people around them who haven't been so privileged. They may just not understand less-privileged people's lives and

---

[53] We often include verbal negotiation skills as part of the mental aspects of the training, including cross-cultural conflict resolution skills.

challenges—especially if those people are from a strange or different culture, or a much lower socio-economic status. Culture shock-generated disrespect for people in lower economic, educational and social strata by the "educated" has caused America more problems overseas than almost anything else.

The concept of moral values, intellectual learning plus positive action is a formula for ethical behavior in non-warrior situations. As we have explored, the difference between right and wrong, morality and immorality, is not often a matter of life and death. Sometimes it is just a matter of getting a reasonable balance of concern between self and others in order to live a good life. Getting that good balance between self and others—and maintaining it through a practice regimen—is the art of living the "good life."

For the Ethical Warrior, the moral inclination to protect life is not just an idea. It is what they do. Warrior Ethics are moral actions—in defense of others. Unfortunately, that aspect is unexamined or missing from much modern day martial arts training. It was absent from mine, until I stumbled upon an important secret—by mistake.

The Technique *IS* the Ethic

As a break from my day job, I often teach martial arts seminars on the weekend. But they almost invariably are at schools that practice the same martial art that I do. Martial arts are rather parochial; people tend to pick one that they like and stick with it. They are rarely interested in another style or another teacher. So it was very unusual for me to get a call one day from a hard-style karate teacher in Florida asking me if I would come down to teach a seminar at his school. Evidently, he had heard about me or met me somewhere, but I didn't really know him. I wasn't enthusiastic about it. My martial arts approach was very different from their style, and I didn't want to get involved in a possibly contentious environment. I was afraid that I would show them something and they would counter with the typical and predictable, "yeah, but in our style we do it *this* way." The fellow was very persistent, however. I finally said, half in jest, "OK, keep an eye on the Weather Channel; when you see it snowing in New Jersey, call me and ask me again." Sure enough, months later, while it was snowing briskly outside my office, I received a call. "How would you like to come to Florida?" I went.

My first thought was that I had guessed right. This group was going to be a tough one. They were all gigantic-looking, dressed in crisp white *do-gi* martial arts uniforms and were snapping these frighteningly powerful punches and kicks at each other. One of the guys, I think, was even nicknamed "Meat!" I thought to myself, "Geez, what am I going to teach *these* guys?" But there I was. I knew that if I tried to show them anything remotely like what they already knew, they would probably resist and start with the comparisons. I was desperately looking for the right approach. Then I got an idea. I said, "You already know how to punch in your own defense, but if you had to protect someone else, you could punch this (different) way." I broke them up into threes and taught them how to strike my way in defense of others. They were intrigued, and they tried it. "Whew," I said to myself, "it's working." But then something totally unexpected happened: They started talking and laughing. It wasn't fool around laughing, it was the laughter of joy. They absolutely loved protecting others. My head was swimming; I had hit on something important, but I wasn't quite sure what it was.

At the end of the seminar, Meat came up to me and he had tears in his eyes. "Thank you so much," he said. "I have been doing martial arts for many years, but today, for the first time, I really got the feeling I was looking for when I first started. I felt like the good guy, the protector." Wow. That was it!

Now I teach protecting others all over the world, and the same thing happens. The concept is simple, once you understand it. Make sure that the warrior ethic is *in* the training; in other words, practice martial arts techniques—not only in defense of self—but also in defense of others. In three decades of martial arts training I have been in hundreds of *dojo* (martial arts schools) and have seen thousands of techniques. Reliably, 99.9% of these techniques involve the person protecting him or herself. Where is the balance between self and others in this training methodology? No wonder martial arts in the world practiced as sports are getting more selfish and more violent, and the culture surrounding these martial sports is becoming ruder and cruder. It is fundamentally imbalanced. In order to be true to our nature, training to protect others may be even more important than learning self-defense. Some of us have done personal protection, bodyguarding, etc., yet, martial arts training typically concentrates mostly on defending oneself. Training to protect others can make a tremendously positive difference in the psychological and spiritual attitudes of the warrior.

The martial arts training, when properly taught, works so well because it activates the Dual Life Value. It is taught with a slight skew toward the "others" side of the balance. In most cases, attending to others not only preserves the species, it also bolsters the protector's spirit. The intellectual and physical efforts translate into a spiritual feeling of nobility. Humphrey used to say, "It's character building." This is why the Humphreys always explained to visitors to their schools that STRIKE was part of the values, as opposed to the "body" or physical fitness, portion of the curriculum.

For those martial artists out there who may be interested in learning to protect others, the approach is simple. Use the same techniques you already know, but set up scenarios where someone else is (or some others are) attacking a person that you are protecting. It is interesting, fun, and you can learn a lot about the technicalities of real life-protecting actions. However, here is a vital guideline: *The object is not to fight the "bad guy;" the focus is on defending the victim.* It is a subtle difference, but an important one. As a defender of life, the Ethical Warrior has a moral obligation, commensurate with his skill level, to protect everyone he or she can. That does not mean that you should be hanging out at gas stations waiting for them to be robbed so you can save somebody. But it does mean that you want to be morally, psychologically and physically ready in case you are called on to protect.

And remember, although the Ethical Warrior defends the good guys, anyone would do that if they could. The Ethical Warrior protects the bad guys, too (if possible and if he or she is skilled enough), even if it is only long enough for the police to get there, for the jury to try them, and for the judge to sentence them. Remember, warriors are not vigilantes. Interestingly, the protector sensibility may manifest itself as a more effective physical technique in a spontaneous situation. It also "feels" better because it is ethical.

Following the code of Ethical Warrior, protector of life, can enhance your efficacy out in the cold, cruel world—and not only if you in one of the protector professions. The benefits are available for everyone. It can also improve the quality of life at home, as we will discuss very shortly.

At the beginning of this chapter I told the story of a young Marine being taught a warrior lesson by Robert L. Humphrey. Humphrey had given that young, aggressive Marine officer some unusual "homework." He said, "Jack, tonight when you go out tonight, instead of giving everyone intimidating looks, try this instead: say to yourself 'everyone in this place is a little safer because I am here.'"

Even today, when I walk through the mall, or sit in the subway, or pass through the scary part of town, I wonder if I am confident and secure enough in my values and skills to live that admonition. Can I project an acknowledgment of human equality into the eyes of everyone I meet? Even people who may have behaviors I don't particularly like—perhaps even criminals? Can I separate the relative value of their behavior (which may be good, bad or indifferent) from the absolute, intrinsic value of their life, and remain the protector? Is everyone in my presence truly safer, because I am there? I hope so. Because when I act as an Ethical Warrior, *I* also feel good inside—and more secure. *More* secure when I am the protector? That may sound counter-intuitive, but it is one of the mysterious side benefits of being an Ethical Warrior—you will feel noble and safer yourself, too!

I have shared the story of my epiphany regarding warrior ethics with audiences all over the world, and they have responded positively. The vast majority of them, too, feel that living life as an Ethical Warrior is a "better life." One of the byproducts of telling the story, however, is that people sometimes view me as some kind of sage. When it started to happen, I have to admit, I began to enjoy the accolades and think that they were my due for bringing Humphrey's powerful message to the world. But here is a little secret: It is not difficult to look like an enlightened warrior genius for a few hours or a few days in front of a sympathetic audience. It does not mean you are one.

And so, of course, it happened. Almost exactly 16 years after that first homework assignment from Professor Humphrey. I learned that I was not yet the Ethical Warrior I thought I was.

Epiphany in New Jersey

Dr. Humphrey was visiting my home. We were doing a seminar that combined warrior ethics and combative skills in one moral-physical lesson. That would be the next day. But it was Friday and I was still working my day job in North Jersey nearly 60 miles from my house. It was March, it was raining and sleeting, and I had already had a bad day at work. I couldn't wait to get out of the office. I finally headed out on to the icy roads and into the nerve-wracking traffic. People were driving very poorly, smacking into

each other and driving off the road into ditches.
Over the course of that miserable drive on the icy
roads, I grew more and more tense. It took me
about two-and-a-half hours to get home—about
twice as long as normal. When I finally arrived,
got out of the car and walked up to my front door,
I just about had smoke coming out of my ears.
(Ever had a day like that?)

Imagine this scene as I opened the door and
walked into my house: Dr. Humphrey was sitting
to my left on the couch in the living room with my
two little kids crawling all over him laughing and
screaming. My wife was to my right, in the kitchen
cooking and singing. And I'm standing there after
having had this horrific day, and for some reason,
the whole scene just pissed me off! I felt, "I'm glad
everyone else is having such a great time while I
am out bringing home the bacon." I remember
standing there with a strange torn feeling and I
must have had that look on my face again. Dr.
Humphrey looked sharply up at me from the
couch and said, "Get out!" Get out? I thought to
myself, "Wait a minute, this is my house." He
said, again: "GET OUT!"

So I got out.

I walked out the door, and I remember
standing on the porch in the sleet. He soon came
out and looked at me, sternly at first, and then
kindly. He said, "Jack, do you know what was

going on in this house before you walked in the door? Everybody was waiting in joyous anticipation of you coming home. We couldn't wait for you to get home, because we were all going to have dinner and be together and enjoy the evening. And you walked in looking like that and in three seconds you broke everybody's heart in this house. Is that what you were trying to do, there…Mr. 'Ethical Warrior'?"

I was ashamed and felt about an inch tall. He went on to say, "If you're really going to be a warrior, these are the people that you need to protect—especially their feelings and their hearts."

And that's where the last component of "The Warrior Creed" came from.

When I return home,
everyone is happy I am there.
"It's a better life!"

I have told that story all over the world and, regardless of culture, everybody seems to understand and resonate with it. I was leading a large martial arts seminar in a South American country several years ago. It was going very well, despite the fact that everything had to be translated from English into Spanish. The seminar was very physical, of course, but I used the bonding feeling that "shared adversity" creates and sat everyone down at various points of the three day event to tell the values stories. Not surprisingly, the stories lose nothing in translation. People are people everywhere.

At the very end I told the group that I was going to leave them with some "homework" and told them the Warrior Creed stories. Everyone seemed very touched, and I felt very good about it. We took a lot of pictures and said good bye. As I gathered my gear to leave I was approached by a nicely dressed middle-aged couple. They had obviously not been participants of the seminar, but they asked in fairly good English if they could speak with me. They were crying. I said of course, a little concerned and wondering to myself what it was all about. They explained: "Our son was at your seminar all weekend and enjoyed it very much. We came to pick him up to take him to dinner...and break the news to him that we were going to get a divorce." You can imagine my reaction. I was immediately saddened, of course, but wondered what this had to do with me. Then they said, "We got here a little early and heard your story about the Warrior Creed." They looked at each other and continued, "And we have decided to stay together." Now we were all crying.

The challenge is to always remember to protect our loved ones and families, along with everyone else. If you think about it, aren't they the *most* vulnerable to our mean or disrespectful behavior? There is an old saying: "You always hurt the ones you love," and we know that after a difficult tour of duty—or even a tough day at the office—it is common to bring the stress and fear home with us where it is "safer" to dissipate it. But the Ethical Warrior recognizes that the work is not done when he or she comes "home from the wars." Rather, job #1 is just starting. That is, to protect and defend the ones he or she loves the most. So we encourage you to try the Warrior Creed on for size.

Wherever I go,
everyone is a little bit safer because I am there.
Wherever I am,
anyone in need has a friend.
When I return home,
everyone is happy I am there.
It's a better life!

Living by this simple admonition may take us all a long way toward decreasing domestic problems and creating happier families. In many ways, living the last part of the Warrior Creed is the most difficult. But if we can do it, it is truly a better life.

Afterword
Kill Socrates

"Far from ever doing any man a wrong or rendering him more wicked, [I] have rather profited those who conversed with me by teaching them, without reward, every good thing that lay in my power."
- Socrates, Plato's Apologia

"To right the unrightable wrong / To love, pure and chaste from afar / To try, when your arms are too weary / To reach the unreachable star."
- Don Quixote de La Mancha [singing]

"Start with a faulty premise, and no matter how smart you are, you may end up with a faulty conclusion."
- Me. I just made that up.

Shortly before Humphrey's death, he was invited to speak at Drew University on the subject of values. It was there that he retold the story, mentioned previously, of the Japanese prisoner and how saving his enemy also saved his humanity. But something else very significant happened that day. While I was driving him to the conference, I mentioned casually that I had just been interviewed by Black Belt magazine, a widely read martial arts periodical. They were mostly interested in Japanese martial arts techniques, but I had been able to include a little about the Life Value by steering the interview discussion to the topic of "protecting others." Suddenly Humphrey's ears seemed to perk up. "So," he asked, "what did you say?" "The usual stuff," I replied casually. Suddenly, he got very serious. "No, Jack, what exactly did you say?" I was taken aback by his tone, and a little bit insulted. After all, I had been his associate for almost 17 years and had played a big part in producing his book. I knew how to represent the Life Value concept. So I answered huffily, "What's the matter, don't you trust me?"

"Pull over!" Humphrey ordered.

He may have been in his 70's but he could still be intimidating...so I pulled over. And there we were, sitting on the shoulder of Route 287, with cars whizzing by, and Humphrey looking at me with as stern a look as I have ever seen on his face. Here is what he said: "Jack, this is not some kind of intellectual game so that you can be entertaining in a magazine. This is of critical importance in the real world. When I was dealing with real conflict, and I said something one way, it might stop the violence and killing; if I said it another way, I could actually make the violence and killing worse. So, no, I don't trust you. I don't trust myself. So what did you say?"

One of the nerve-wracking aspects of writing this book is the fear that I won't be able to convey to the reader how vitally important and subtle the Life Value is for promoting peace and stopping conflict.

These many years after Humphrey's death, I still worry if I am saying the right things in the right way. And also if it is the right time to say it. Like all great lessons, the values stories and the Life Value philosophy are taught most effectively in context. If this is not the right time to write this book, it may not connect with people and I will not have done any good. I have said repeatedly that I almost never present the Dual Life Value concept as an intellectual proposition, but instead use stories and physical training as my delivery mechanism. So, as I finish this book I admit it—I feel a little anxious about the whole thing.

As a young man in the thrall of coming to understand the Life Value, I was amazed at Bob Humphrey's patience. I often urged him to do this or do that to spread his Life Value concept so that it could help make the world a more peaceful and happier place. I personally wrote letters and sent many copies of his vital book, "Values For A New Millennium," to corporate, government and military leaders—including every president of the United States since the early 1990's when the book was first published. Humphrey didn't discourage me, but he showed little sense of urgency. His attitude, to me, was incomprehensible. Didn't he see the world was still a very dangerous place, and that his theories and peace-making skills could help? It frustrated the heck out of me. Finally, one day he took me aside like he had done so many times over the years and said,

"Jack, you can't sell this stuff. Just put it out there, and when things get bad enough, they'll come looking for us. If people are not yet 'getting' what we are saying, it just means they haven't tried everything else yet. The timing has to be right." Wow. If you didn't know Humphrey, you might think he was a real cynic, but he was just telling it like it was—and is. People are moral—they know when something is wrong. But they often have great difficulty being ethical—knowing what to do about it and then doing it—until the time is right.

In my experience, it is even more peculiar. Even when people finally get around to doing something about a serious social or economic problem, sometimes they do just enough to make the problem get a little better, and then they go right back to what they were doing. After learning about Humphrey's accomplishments in depth, I was amazed that he wasn't more famous. It turned out that much of Humphrey's work was done quietly and sometimes secretly. The issues he dealt with were so sensitive, and often potentially politically embarrassing, that he had to act very carefully behind the scenes to stop conflict. He worked on problems that no one wanted to admit even existed. Often, he would solve a very serious, cross-cultural mystery that was causing conflict, violence and even death. But once the problem started to subside, no one ever bothered to ask Humphrey the most obvious question: "How did you do it?" No, they were just happy that the problem seemed to go away and they wanted to forget about it.

Humphrey's value-based approach, itself, was also treated as suspect. He was attacked by some who thought his approach was some kind of "psychological warfare." Others considered his secular approach an affront to religious beliefs. Humphrey laughed at that perspective. More often than not, after people were exposed to the Life Value theory, they became *more* religious. The Life Value view of human nature felt so right and natural that it actually gave people more faith in the God who had blessed us with it.

But, people definitely have problems with radical new ideas. And, in a way, the Life Value is radical, although it is not new—it's just Humphrey's articulation of it that is new. The activation and reinforcement methodologies are also new, but not the Life Value itself. We are saying that all life is equal, and that you have to protect and respect everyone; even enemies, if possible. That admonition is not new; it is thousands of years old. However, we propose that the self-others balancing act is an inherent ability in all of us, that it comes from within, and that we have to have enough freedom to exercise it. Outside influences, such as laws, rules, cultural mores, great literature and stories, scientific discoveries, parental guidance, mentorship, etc., can help and guide us, but, every externally acquired value first must be qualified by the superseding Life Value. Further, it is ultimately up to each of us, individually, to attain a reasonable, balanced regard between self and others. In order to be able to do that, we must be free of unnecessary controls. Yet, with all that freedom, there must be enough outside, *necessary* controls to make sure we have the means to address the actions of those of us who "lose" the balance.

As mentioned in the Introduction, "saving the world is like mowing the lawn; you have to do it about once a week." Humphrey's warnings went even further. He often said that getting individual people to resonate with the Life Value was easy, it was the institutional change needed to better reflect the Life Value in our society, government, businesses and other large organizations that was by far the hardest challenge. He was referring to the ancient and real problem of the "Kill Socrates Syndrome." Like the saying: "I'm not paranoid, people are just out to get me," he often reminded me that people *did* kill Socrates—and also Jesus Christ, John the Baptist, Cicero, Ghandi and Martin Luther King for their "radical" ideas. In our own age of confused relativism, I have encountered people who have purposely misrepresented what I have said and even attacked me in writing for teaching "objective values" (mainly human equality). And don't forget Humphrey's experience with the friendly group of young State Department and United States Agency for International Development officers in the "Hunting Story" country, who "explained" to him (quite sincerely and quite mistakenly) that Jefferson and Washington had invented the "equality concept" in order to raise cannon-fodder armies for their land-grabbing American Revolution.

For you change agents out there, here are three factors that allowed Humphrey to continue his efforts in the face of institutional inertia:

1. He would teach the attitude-changing values anecdotally without explaining the theoretical guidelines. (Although I have "risked" writing out the pure theory to the best of my ability in this book, please remember that I usually don't use the theory to activate the Life Value in my audiences; I use the *values stories* and the *martial arts*.)
2. Since the values-education stopped violence and sabotage, it was welcomed by most practical-minded administrators, bureaucrats and military commanders.
3. The real saving factor was in the embedded philosophy of the average person. People all over the world did not reject the value of the inalienable right to life and the concept of human equality; rather, they accepted them as obvious truths, too long neglected.

Isn't that is what is happening in the "Arab Spring?" I would propose that the "awakening" isn't a sudden desire to be *culturally* like the West; rather it is a desire to have what we Americans sometimes take for granted: respect for their lives and the lives of their loved ones as equal human beings, and not pawns of others. It's important to note that not all the participants in the protests and uprisings are Arab. The movement is a reflection of a feeling shared by *all* people everywhere: "Don't tread on me."

Most of the young people from whom Humphrey received program critiques—both in the military and later in some pretty tough public schools—remarked that the validity of the Life Value was something they had always known but just had never been able to put into words. In truth, it was something that they felt and was a part of them—subsurface but aching to be expressed and activated. The fact was, Humphrey found, that almost every young "common-folk" American—most with only a high-school education—seemed to be hungry for the moral awakening inspired by those values-lectures and discussions. It was no different with people overseas—in many cases, they were even *hungrier* for the lessons.

I have found the same reaction from most military, law enforcement and martial arts people with whom I have worked. The more difficult audiences, believe it or not, are highly educated people with money. Perhaps it is because their wealth and relative security mean that they are often so far removed from the realities of life and death that they get intellectually "wrapped around the axle" by something as straightforward and simple as the Dual

Life Value. Clearly anything as "radical" as the Life Value is sure to change the paradigm of the relativistic philosophies that underpin the educational theories used in many of our schools—especially universities.

Then there is this: an insightful friend read one of my articles on "The Ethical Warrior" in the Marine Corps Gazette and remarked that Al Qaeda wasn't going to be happy with me and that I should be careful. Huh? I remember thinking to myself that my friend was being a little melodramatic. But he explained, "Listen, you are teaching Marines how to better win hearts and minds overseas, our enemies are not going to like it, so watch out!" Hmmm... interesting advice.

So I pay attention, but I keep going. I think that the power of the Life Value can do a lot to help America, not just overseas, but here at home. Hopefully, we have a chance to get past the Kill Socrates Syndrome and consider positive change because most Americans seem to see that our society and institutions are ripe for it.

Humphrey often explained to me the wisdom of a tolerant attitude toward the infuriating opposition to constructive, fresh ideas and approaches for conflict resolution. As any investigative scientist knows, you fail constantly on the way to success. Hence, no matter who obstructs and causes you to fail in this change-agent business, if you fail at first, you must claim the failure as your own fault. Why? Because it is, and that admission also serves you best. Human nature is strongly with you in activating the Life Value. So if you were right and still failed, it was because you were not smart enough to overcome the natural inclination against change. Understand that the Kill Socrates Syndrome, that knee-jerk opposition to change, is quite human. Change can be dangerous. We fear it. We have good reason for this concern: For at least a million years certain changes, and their unforeseen consequences, have led to human deaths.

You will certainly need patience and maturity for the challenge of trying to activate acknowledgement of the Dual Life Value as *the* core value for peace and well-being in virtually every aspect of life: work, play, education, peacekeeping, and even within the family. Why? Because, especially if you start to succeed, you *will* encounter the Kill Socrates syndrome—possibly in the form of character-assassination, if not actual physical attacks.

The following three-part regimen is a guideline to prepare yourself for the challenges:

1. A clarified understanding of the nature of values, morals and ethics—the Life Value;
2. A ready collection of values-stories to help you break through to the emotions, and;
3. The moral and physical courage to help you be ethical—even under duress.

In our increasingly soft society, even with highly physical Marines, the biggest barrier to overcome is the physical aspect of the moral/mental/physical formula. Yet, the physical component is all but indispensable. To ethically upgrade society, civilian and military educators must teach people to be willing and able, unarmed and individually, to speak up against immoral behavior. That includes physically protecting the innocent when necessary. But this social responsibility for "involvement" is now weak if not rejected in our culture. "Don't get involved." "Don't take the law into your own hands." "What am *I* supposed to do?" "I'll get sued." In the mid-1950's and before, the social responsibility for life-protecting involvement was very strong on any downtown street in our nation of small towns. From that strong social responsibility, along with our culture of "rugged individualism," America became a great nation. The rebuilding of that unifying social responsibility is critical. Today, except for a slight bump after 9/11, we seem to be going in the other direction, with increasing polarization, an overemphasis on "diversity" (relative values), severe economic problems, a loss of respect for America overseas and other seemingly insurmountable problems. Many responsible citizens can see no solution short of profound change, maybe even revolution. Yet, I believe that if we reaffirm our Life Value—respect for life and human equality—the problems will lessen and issues will be addressed more fairly and amicably. They may even just fade away.

Historically, America is facing these odds: No nation in the history of the world has reached our status of leadership and stayed there. Those are bad odds, indeed. The Dual Life Value and the code of the Ethical Warrior give us a chance, but, the challenge is tremendous and clear. It is also exciting and worthy. And it can start with us. That is why I wrote this book. It was not to change institutions from the top down. It was to help clarify and activate our—yours and my—personal moral behavior from the ground up, one person at a time, if necessary. If you are reading these last sentences, that may mean you are one of those people. I hope so; we need you.

Acknowledgements

As usual in a book like this, there are scores of people who have contributed in many ways to its creation. At the top of the list is the Humphrey family—their patience and confidence in my ability to articulate and share Robert L. Humphrey's life and work has made me feel like one of the family. Thank you all beyond words.

Next are Masaaki Hatsumi and the scores of *buyu* (martial arts friends) that I have met and trained with all over the world for 30 years. *Domo arigato*!

There have been many great Marine leaders of varying rank who are responsible for the current success of the Marine Corps Martial Arts Program and the Ethical Warrior concept—too many to list here, but several should be acknowledged, including: Colonel George Bristol, General Kevin Nally, LtCol Pat Beckett, and my good friend LtCol (ret.) Joseph Shusko. Two other great Marines from the program who have become good friends are Sergeant Major (ret.) Brian Pensak and Master Gunnery Sergeant (ret.) Shane Franklin. Hoplologist Hunter Armstrong has also been a valuable resource for the program.

Resolution Group International (www.rgi.co) is a company I started to bring the training methodology of the Ethical Warrior and Ethical Protector to law enforcement organizations and businesses. You can find a list of our associates and their credentials on the Bio page on the website. Please take a look; they are all awesome and professional examples of the Ethical Warrior and I am extremely privileged to be working with them. Do train with some or all of them if you get the opportunity!

In terms of the book, itself, there are several interested friends who have read all or part of the manuscript and given me great advice. They include: Rob Humphrey, Galen Humphrey, Jess Humphrey, Jim Morganelli, Margarita Tapia, Joe Shusko, Brian Pensak, Bruce Gourlie, Jeff Morrison, Ken Cassie, Geoff Metcalf, Mike Olivier, Bob Drury, Sam Awar, Brad Miner, Tom Cline, Jim Manley, Josh Sager, Kat Grausso, Gary Klugiewicz, Bob Willis, Joe Finder, Neil Doherty and Steven Pinker.

Finally, I want to thank my family for all of the love and support over the years. It isn't easy having a warrior in the family. I would especially like to thank my Dad, Gene Hoban. Without his encouragement, I would never have taken up the challenge of being a United States Marine Corps Officer, and this journey along the warrior path may never have started.

About The Author

Jack Hoban served as a U.S. Marine Corps officer and is a long time practitioner of martial arts. He assisted in the creation of the Marine Corps Martial Arts Program and remains a subject matter expert for the program. Hoban has led more than 500 workshops and seminars around the world addressing universities, government and private organizations on ethics and martial arts, including the Federal Bureau of Investigation (FBI) and the New York Police Department (NYPD). He was a longtime associate of the late Robert L. Humphrey, noted conflict resolution specialist and author of "Values for a New Millennium." Hoban is also a master instructor in the Japanese Bujinkan Budo Taijutsu martial arts system. Jack can be reached through his website at www.livingvalues.com.

About The Training

Resolution Group International (RGI) was formed by experienced military, law enforcement and education professionals to provide a specialized approach to conflict resolution and conflict resolution training. RGI's synergistic formula of ethical, verbal and physical skills is unique. RGI works with the military, various law enforcement agencies, non-governmental organizations and corporate businesses to develop Ethical Warriors and Ethical Protectors. RGI's website is www.rgi.co.